SCENIC
RAILWAY
MODELLING

compiled and edited by
MICHAEL ANDRESS

PSL Patrick Stephens, Wellingborough

A Rhaetian Railway 'Crocodile' emerges from a tunnel and rolls straight onto a bridge crossing Rheinfalle Gorge high above the river below. The gorge is a spectacular scenic feature at one end of the HO scale metre gauge 'Die Bernhardinbahn' layout.

First published 1985

British Library Cataloguing in Publication Data

Scenic railway modelling.
   1. Railroads—Models
  I. Andress, Michael
  625.1'9   TF197

   ISBN 0-85059-711-0

Patrick Stephens Limited is part of the Thorsons Publishing Group.

Text photoset in 9 on 10pt Times by MJL Typesetting, Hitchin, Herts. Printed in Great Britain on 115 gsm Fineblade coated cartridge, and bound, by Butler & Tanner Limited, Frome, Somerset, for the publishers, Patrick Stephens Limited, Denington Estate, Wellingborough, Northants, NN8 2QD, England.

Contents

Introduction 4

Scenery design by Richard Wyatt 5

Scenic landscape modelling by Andy McMillan 12

A planning model by Michael Andress 17

Lee-on-the-Solent by Colin Hayward 21

Ipsley Circle—'Coombe Mellin' river scene by David Simmonite 27

Modelling Rheinfalle Gorge by David and Mike Polgaze 33

Modelling small scenes by David and Mike Polgaze 39

Eitomo—an East African narrow gauge (009) model railway by Howard Coulson 46

A model dock by David Andress 55

Rock faces by Richard Wyatt 61

Foxes Farmhouse by Andy McMillan 71

Low relief modelling by Bob Petch 75

Canal modelling by Michael Andress 84

Model a miniature railway by Michael Andress 93

Introduction

From very simple beginnings in the early days of railway modelling the scenic setting has become a major feature of most model railway layouts. Not only have many new construction techniques been devised, or acquired from other modelling and craft hobbies, but the whole concept of creating a railway set in its own landscape has developed to give much greater realism and interest. Scenery modelling has also become one of the most popular facets of the railway modelling hobby. This is not surprising. Scenery construction is not difficult and even a beginner can achieve considerable success. The results can be very satisfying both in themselves and in the way in which they enhance the realism of the railway models. Also it is on the scenic side that the enthusiast can most easily give his or her layout its own character and individuality.

In compiling this book I have endeavoured to select articles covering a wide range of different scenic modelling topics ranging from general planning principles to the addition of small details. The standard of realism of model railways today has been influenced considerably by the idea that the scenery should not merely be added as a final touch to fill in any gaps, but should be planned from the beginning as an integral part of the layout. Dick Wyatt, whose narrow gauge layout was featured on TV in one of the 'Two Ronnies' shows, and Andy McMillan, a professional modeller, present their ideas on this important subject while a third article on this theme suggests the use of small planning models as design aids.

Much of the realism of scenic modelling comes from the effective blending of the various elements in the scene. I am very pleased to be able to include articles from Colin Hayward, David Simmonite, David and Mike Polglaze, and Howard Coulson covering the complete scenic setting for a layout or section of a layout. The geographical locations for the prototypes modelled range from the South Coast of England to Switzerland to East Africa. Though very different in character they all show a high standard of scenic modelling.

A recently developed concept is to model the landscape as a series of independent but related scenes. This very effective approach is well illustrated by David and Mike Polglaze on their Swiss narrow gauge line and by Howard Coulson on his East African layout.

The remainder of the book deals with a number of more specific scenic modelling subjects. Dick Wyatt gives advice on various methods for modelling realistic rock faces, Andy McMillan explains why and how he modelled a farm scene and Bob Petch describes the construction of an extensive low relief town scene for his layout. Further articles detail the building of a small dock, provide information for canal modelling and suggest modelling a miniature railway as an unusual but appropriate scenic feature.

In scenic work, perhaps more than in any other branch of railway modelling, there is no one and only right way to do it. There are many different methods and techniques all of which will produce good results. In this book we can see how different modellers have tackled various aspects of scenery design and construction and I hope that readers will find this interesting and informative.

I am grateful to all the contributors for sharing with us their ideas and experiences in scenery modelling. I would also like to thank all those modellers who have allowed me to use photographs of their scenic work to illustrate various points in this book.

MICHAEL ANDRESS

Scenery design

Richard Wyatt

Railway modelling as a hobby is probably unique in the wide range of skills that can be applied by its devotees. The enormous variety of models and layouts that ensues, ensures that the personal desires and abilities of an individual will always be welcome within some branch of the hobby. The dedicated model engineer will spend much of his time turning out locos and stock, others will enjoy model building construction and civil engineering. The electrical and operational sides call on a totally different range of abilities, and there is no limit to the circuitry that can be introduced to advantage by the electrical enthusiast, not to mention the depth to which timetable working can be developed. For the artist with no great mechanical or electrical abilities, the scenic setting can be his expression within the hobby, the trains themselves being no more than equal in importance (and probably less so) to the landscape through which the trains run.

If a group layout is being considered, the ideal would be to draw together specialists in each of the various skills (many people are good at more than one task) under the strong leadership of someone who has a clear idea of what the group is trying to achieve, but who can maintain a balance between the technical and artistic side. This is difficult to obtain, and many groups tend towards technical brilliance while being weaker on the artistic side.

The lone modeller, however, is in an entirely different position. If, at the end of the day, he wants a reasonable looking model railway, he will have to utilise something of each of the skills involved, including areas in which he lacks confidence, unless he can call on outside help. Most lone modellers will not feel expert in many, if any, particular skills, but they have one large advantage over a group. Any layout built by one person is an expression of his own personality and the way he sees things, and for that reason has a consistency and atmosphere not always found in group layouts. Often this factor far outweighs any technical shortcomings or shortcuts taken due to time and cash factors and is probably most evident when the modeller is artistically rather than technically minded. This is because it is easier to express personality through scenic work where choice is infinite, than in modelling prototype items where choice is limited. Ideally, then, the modeller wants to create realistic trains running on a realistic railway through realistic stations and, above all, in a realistic setting. Achieving all these will usually produce a satisfactory result, notwithstanding that the ability to obtain prototypical accuracy in each area, though desirable, may be beyond the skill, time or funds of the individual building the model.

From the foregoing, it is clear that scenery should be considered right from the start when planning a model railway and is as much part of the design concept as track layout, buildings, period and type of trains. Too many layouts have all the track laid and many of the buildings

Fig 1 Example of a cut and fill system and a railway built on a shelf.

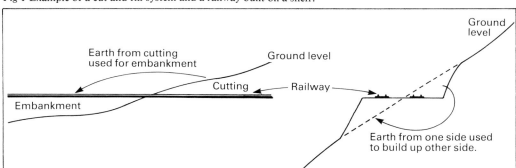

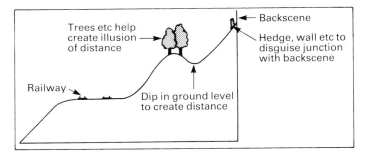

Left *Fig 2* Creating a sense of distance between railway track and backscene.

Below *Fig 3* Ways of disguising roads and rivers at rear edge of baseboard.

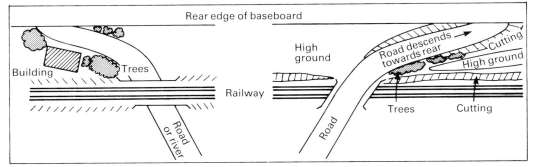

completed before much thought is given to scenery, with the end result that the railway does not look part of the landscape and realism is lost. In many cases the track is laid on a flat surface which is fitted directly onto a frame and gives no real opportunity for the contours to dip below the level of the track so that all scenic features, hills etc, have the tendency to appear 'stuck on'.

A look at any building site will show that some modification to the landscape is required for most construction work and railway construction is no exception. Only in very rare cases was the railway laid on top of the unmodified landscape. Usually the 'cut and fill' system was employed, where embankments used approximately the same amount of material as that removed from nearby cuttings so that no material had to be moved to or

from the site. Obviously one does not need to imitate exactly this principle in model form but it should be borne in mind. Thus, we see that any railway construction, whether plain track or a station, will break into the natural line of the landscape by being either above or below it, or on a shelf cut into the hillside. This may be by only a few feet, and, after a few decades, the growth of trees and bushes may disguise the fact, but it is still there and should be acknowledged when planning our model.

There are a number of other ways in which the planning of scenery can assist in creating realism in a model. Much has been said by others about the use of visual breaks such as tunnels and road overbridges to create a sense of distance in the railway and these are also very valuable to

Left *Lilla crosses the viaduct to Llanymawddwy station. Though the height of the railway above the river is not much more than 10cm the feature is still large enough to dominate this end of the layout. (Photograph by R. Wyatt).*
Right *Llanymawddwy station has a realistic blend of interesting structures suggesting that there have been additions and alterations over the years. The natural contours of the station area have been 'cut and filled' to provide a level site with a retaining wall between the station and the road falling away in front.*

disguise the circular appearance of a continuous run. Besides using tunnels and bridges, curves can be effectively hidden in deep cuttings or behind clumps of trees or groups of buildings. When planning the scenery, it is worth remembering that, within reason, the greater the number of times the train disappears into tunnels and cuttings, under bridges, and behind trees or buildings, and reappears, the greater the apparent distance run. Obviously, it is not a good idea to make tunnels too short, a train sticking out of both ends of a tunnel destroys any advantage gained.

Roads can do much to link the different parts of a layout together into a coherent whole and every effort should be made to give the roads a reason for their existence so they will actually appear to go from somewhere to somewhere else. Like rivers, roads should be allowed for in the early design stage to avoid the 'stuck-on afterwards' effect, and consideration given as to how and where the roads will cross the railway lines. From the foregoing it will be seen that there are obvious advantages in the road crossing over the railway, but there are advantages in roads passing beneath the railway also, trains crossing bridges can be a very attractive feature. For a road to pass beneath the railway, the track will, of course, need to be laid above baseboard level. When a road or river goes off the edge of the baseboard, rather than leading it straight over the edge, consider bending it to the left or right behind features such as hills, buildings or trees, so that the end of the road or river is disguised from normal viewing angles. A sense of depth between the railway lines and the edge of the baseboard can be created by allowing the scenery to rise and dip in front of the backscene, this tends to make the backscene seem further away than it actually is. The transition between the three dimensional scenery and two dimensional backscene is helped by installing hedges, walls, trees and buildings directly in front of the backscene.

If we are to create a realistic and plausible model, some thought must be directed towards the area in which the prototype for our model is set. In many cases there will be some freedom of choice as it will not be intended to model an exact prototype, but this does not mean that anything goes. An early decision needs to be made as to the general image aimed for, whether through pastoral countryside, amid wild mountainous scenery, near rivers or the coast, urban or industrial and so on. With a general idea in mind, every effort should be made to visit suitable locations, not just for a quick drive through, but to spend time and look closely. Resorting to magazine pictures, photographs and memory is very much second best as it is only by visits to typical locations that we will get the 'feel' of the prototype that needs to be interpreted in model form in order to create atmosphere. Clearly, when modelling a specific prototype, the only suitable site is the actual location of the prototype even though it may be much altered. It is surprising how much atmosphere remains around even after track and buildings have gone, and also, of course, one can see how the chosen site fitted in with the landscape as a whole, something which photographs frequently do not show, and yet essential when considering backscenes. Those of us whose model is based on a particular part of the country or type of scenery rather than a specific prototype are not forced to travel to one particular location for scenic research, but visits to 'typical' sites are still invaluable to try to visualise how the railway would fit in with, and affect, the landscape and to observe the small details which typify a particular area and which give so much extra realism when added to the model.

By this time, and probably long before, the modeller will have realised that the large scale scenic effects created by the natural landscape are

Duke *pulls through Llanymawddwy station with a goods train while the railcar* Colossus *with a brake van in tow waits to leave. The goods shed and goods yard can be seen behind. (Photograph by R. Wyatt).*

The railbus Odin *crosses the bridge over the small stream. The trees have been realistically grouped giving a natural appearance.*

going to occupy far more space than he has at his disposal. The rolling sweep of Wiltshire, the Downs of Kent and Sussex, the ruggedness of North Wales are all too vast to be modelled even in the smallest scales without an enormous amount of space, and representation of these features is usually restricted to the backscene. An acre will occupy about 3ft × 2ft 6in in 4mm scale, so it can be seen that all but the largest layouts will be no bigger than a smallish field.

It is now that the significance of location visits becomes clear as it is necessary to get beneath the general landscape into the more detailed features of the immediate location (say within 100 yards in each direction) and allow the characteristics of the area to impress themselves on the sub-conscious. Because the unusual rather than the typical sticks in the conscious mind, a notebook is essential to record information, preferably from several different locations in our chosen area. Information that needs to be recorded would

include details of the lie of the land, whether smooth or irregular, verges to the roads and fencing to both roads and railway, building style and materials, size of fields and type of enclosure (hedgerow, dry stone wall, fence), types of crops, trees and bushes, grouping and number of trees, type of road surface, condition of roads and whether straight or winding, and so on. If there is a stream or river, are the banks steep or gentle? Wooded, grassy or rocky? Is the stream shallow and fast flowing or deep and slow moving? Is the bottom muddy or stony? Rough sketches are often more informative than written notes to record details even if you have little ability in sketching. There is a vast amount of information that can be collected and it is not advisable to commit anything to memory as it is surprising what cannot be recalled at the required time. Even if you think you have noted everything, there will still be gaps. I found that the most valuable visit that I made to the valley on which my layout is

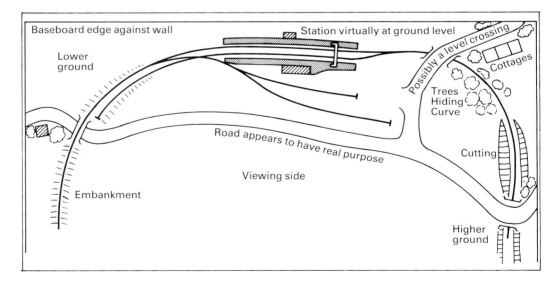

modelled, was the one made after I was well under way with construction and more aware of what I did not know.

Having decided on the theme of the scenic part of our model and with a notebook stuffed with relevant information, together with a selection of suitable photographs, we are now ready to devise a plan for the track layout and basic scenery. If the model is situated in an area of gently undulating landscape, the illusion of reality is enhanced if there is a general trend of slope from one end of the model to the other, with the railway line partly on an embankment, partly in a cutting. Where the landscape is more broken up, the general sloping trend can be maintained, but with much more irregular features in between, and possibly, depending on location, rock outcrops. Before any trees, fences, buildings, etc, are added, the general character of the countryside through which our railway runs can be evident from the lay of the land in the model. If the trackbed has been laid a few inches above baseboard level and the ground allowed to flow above and below track level, the railway will, even at this stage, look as though it has been built into the landscape, and not vice-versa as is often the case.

Once the basic contours of the scenery are in place, work can start on adding the features which will give the model a character and personality of its own, and link it closely to the area in which the model is set, something which, if done well, will be recognisable to the informed onlooker. While the approximate positions of roads, rivers, buildings, etc, will have been known and allowed for before the foundation scenery was laid down, the eye will now be able to appraise the situation better and any route or positional modifications made at this time. As the scenery is worked up by the addition of more features, the model will gradually blossom into an expression of the image that is in the modeller's mind. Although many exist in the real world, the modeller would be well advised to avoid too many of the scenic anomalies that are so tempting to include. More than one or two oddities in the limited space at one's disposal will distract the eye of the viewer from the main theme of the model and confuse the style and image which the modeller is attempting to create. It seems to be a rule when modelling, that conviction of accuracy and authenticity of certain features such as roads and rivers, is achieved more by these being modelled and painted in the manner that the majority of viewers think that they should appear, instead of going to great pains to obtain an exact likeness. Take roads for instance, the surface of which is a blend of greys, browns, blues etc, with odd

Left *Fig 4* Rural scene incorporating some of the ideas in the text.

Right *The Single Fairlie* Gowrie *waits at the head of a passenger train at Aber Rhiwlech station. The natural groupings and positioning of figures, animals and other details enhances the overall effect.*

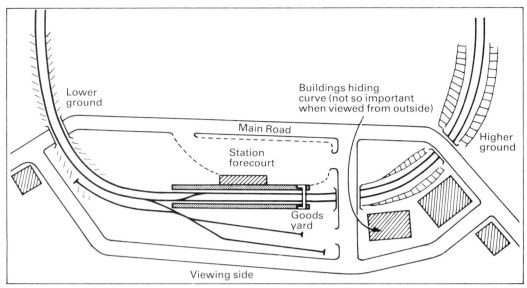

Fig 5 An urban or industrial scene incorporating some of the same ideas.

repaired patches in a different shade. If modelled in this way, it is extremely difficult to produce a road that does not have a patchwork appearance, whereas an overall medium grey/brown, if applied to a suitable textured surface (such as Polyfilla or fine sandpaper), can look far more realistic in model form. Grass, which varies widely in texture and shade, often looks unrealistic if many variations are reproduced in the small area available to the modeller, a single overall colour is usually more convincing.

As features are added to the scenic base, the value of research can be seen. Even if nowhere in particular is being modelled, it is surprising how much we do not know. Things which are part of the everyday scene, if not specifically noted, recede so far into the subconscious as not to be easily recalled, yet it is so necessary for things to appear natural to convince the viewer. The positions and shape of trees, appearance of fences and verges, location of undergrowth, and all those other things which seem so obvious and easy to model convincingly, need to be looked at carefully for the modeller to be able to reproduce them correctly.

Our model will not contain exact copies of the scenic features that we have recorded, but will contain the adaptations required to suit the situation on the model, in many cases features will have to be compressed and simplified. These adaptations will need to be incorporated into the basic plan in such a manner as to correlate with one another and not overwhelm the viewer with conflicting images — much easier to write down than to actually do. For this reason, I would strongly recommend the completion of the scenic foundation over large areas (over the whole layout if that is feasible) including the basic ground cover (grass or whatever), before the individual features (buildings, trees, fences, etc,) are added over the whole layout in something approaching the order in which they would have appeared on the real thing. I feel that trees should be left to near the time when the model is completed for two reasons—firstly, their vulnerability and secondly, the fact that they restrict access to anything in the vicinity. If the whole layout is treated with each feature at one time, the overall effect can be seen much more easily and modified if required. In this way, overcrowding is avoided as the eye will be able to judge when enough has been added. To take an example, the total length of fencing on my own layout is far less than that which is technically possible to enclose roads and railway, but any more would create an overprovision with some ridiculously small enclosed areas. Consequently, the roads are generally left unfenced, with cattle grids included to acknowledge this fact and maintain the link with reality. Still referring to my own layout, I added all the 150 or so trees to the whole layout at once, after roads, buildings and fences, but before people, vehicles, road signs and telegraph poles, and kept adding the trees, either singly or, more usually, in clumps until my eyes told me 'enough'. Incidentally, I then had similar problems to a highway

Above left *This view across the layout shows the undulating scenery which is used to conceal the railway line in the centre, identifiable by the telegraph poles. Trees and vegetation have been arranged to give a natural appearance. The locomotive in the foreground is an old abandoned engine which has been left to rust on a siding.*

Above right *The railcar* Colossus *is reflected in the still water of the lake as it appproaches Llanymawddwy station. Several ducks are just visible on the lake.*

Below left *A view of Llanymawddwy station with the engine shed and yard in the background. Note the neatly modelled road complete with road signs and marker posts. An interesting variety of road vehicles including horse-drawn vehicles and tractors have been employed on the layout.*

Below right *Aber Rhiwech station nestles in a natural hollow and the slopes form a boundary to the scene keeping the viewer's attention on the station.* Mawddwy *is departing with a freight train.*

engineer in siting the road signs clear of trees. Although much of the foregoing has dealt with the model in a countryside setting, the principles remain the same for a model based on an urban or industrial setting, particularly those relating to variation of levels.

To sum up then, for our railway to appear as realistic as possible, there are five main ingredients:

1 We must consider the basic scenic plan at the same time as track layout and allow for scenic work when laying the track.

2 It is essential to ensure that the model presents a cohesive image and not be a collection of unconnected ideas. This is achieved by deciding on the image we want to present or area we want the model to represent, and restricting our modelling to features within that theme.

3 Research is vital to ensure that we are modelling things the way they actually are, and not as we think they are.

4 Construction of the basic scenery in such a way that, as far as possible, the railway appears to have been built after the landscape was there and its route determined by the lay of the land.

5 Working the scenery to near completion in stages over the layout as a whole, leaving only the final detailing to be done on a localised basis. This is not always possible, especially if the layout is being constructed in stages. In this situation each stage is usually brought near completion before commencing the next in which case **1** above is vitally important.

Hopefully, the other articles in this book will give you some ideas about how to put it all into practice.

Scenic landscape modelling

Andy McMillan

One of the great joys of modelling the country-side, including a railway, as opposed to the 'everything inside the railway fence' brigade, is that one learns so much more about life in general. The pleasure gained from looking at a delightfully picturesque cottage is handsomely enhanced by knowing exactly what you are look-ing at. For example, if the end timbers meet in a curved 'A' shape then it is a 'cruck frame', and that will date the cottage around the late 16th Century. It would also tell you, if you looked at how many bays the cottage has, how wealthy the builder was, perhaps even by its shape, its fittings or its position what he did for a living. In fact, the more you study building and the more you get to know about ancient building techniques and availability of various materials in different parts of the country, the greater your understanding of what you are looking at, why it is there, and why it looks the way it does. This may seem quite irrele-vant to a model railway, but if one is looking to fill the odd corner on a model then these questions are often asked in reverse. What do I want there? What will it look like? How shall I build it?

The answer, of course, is to look at real life, but the answer will invariably involve some research, even if that only means browsing through a library book! Most people are aware of the fact that villages came first, and the railway was built to serve them, but more often than not the station was built a mile or more from the village, or at best on the outskirts at one end of town. What more pleasant way of spending a miserable winter evening therefore than looking through a book on village life to find out what sort of people lived outside the village and whereabouts, ie, down in the valleys or up on the hills, discovering the age and history of their houses and then confidently tackling a modelling project to create exactly the scene you want. This is known as the art of scenic landscape modelling and its application to model railways should really begin at the planning stage. The only effective way to plan a model railway is to decide what you want from it when it is finished. The first limitation is that of size. No matter how much room you have the eye can only see so much at once, so depending on how far away from the layout the viewing position is, the golden rule is to break the layout up into visual chunks. Each of these chunks should contain a focal point and visual boundaries to prevent the eye wandering elsewhere. The viewer thus concentrates on a particular area and the wealth of detail you have spent so much time creating can be explored with delight.

Sometime during this process the viewer is dis-

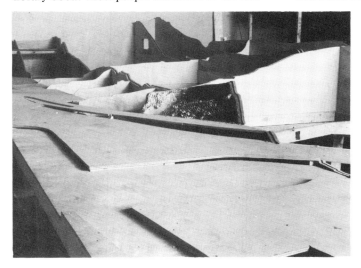

The timber work involved in a large layout. In the foreground is a small dockside area—above it rises the branch line. The station area dis-appears into the left-hand distance. Low hills on the right give a reason for the curvature of the railway and with those in the background help to surround the village area behind the station (A. J. McMillan).

Top right *Here a different and much smaller layout has a main loop of double track in the foreground which will connect with the storage loops placed in the elongated slots in the background. It can be seen how the formers will hold up both track and scenery while at the same time make a sturdy but relatively light structure (A. J. McMillan).*

Centre right *The opposite side of the same layout shows how difficult it can be to fit in scenery when the tracks take up most of the available space. The finished model will benefit greatly from being seen over a strip of green and a few bushes and small trees. Toward the back of the model, an over-steep embankment is necessary, but at the left-hand-side end this will be made into a viaduct which will give the scenery somewhere to go, while being an attractive feature in itself (A. J. McMillan).*

tracted by the movement of a train and the eye immediately goes to it, following it until it stops (at a station), or disappears into a tunnel, a cutting, or under a bridge. The eye will stay rooted to the spot until the last coach or wagon has disappeared, in much the same way as people used to sit and stare at the little white dot disappearing on the old television sets. Then, the movement having gone, the eye will rove about until something interesting is spotted and the cycle begins again. Anyone who has seen a model built in 'visual chunks' will appreciate the fascination it holds for the viewer, whatever the subject. Dioramas in museums are classic examples, particularly those smaller ones in cases. One of the most effective models I ever saw was simply a small fold in the hills with a double track appearing between two fenced off tunnel mouths, a bare halt with a path leading up the hill and petering out, and some lovely models of rusted forlorn engines and tenders just left there to rot. The enclosed 'V' shape of the hills, the path petering out and the blocked off tunnel mouths all concentrated the eye on the forgotten locomotives. There was no escape for the eye, and none for the locos either and thus the sense of dereliction was heightened by the remoteness of the scene.

Not everyone wants to model scenes of pathos of course, so let's look at a few of the rules I use in designing a layout. Forgetting for the moment

Right *The exception that proves the rule. Here the track bed, platform and yard areas are one piece of timber supported by a sub-frame of 3 × 1. It did not seem worth the cost of ply to fit lots of contours when a few offcuts can be added as the scenery is constructed. Note that there is still room for scenery between the operator and the closest tracks even when space is tight. (A. J. McMillan).*

whether we have a main line or a branch, a town scene or a landscape, the first thing is to ensure that there is at least a foot available for scenery all round the track. This includes the ends and the backscene, but not necessarily the front. This may mean that a smaller prototype has to be chosen, or the track layout redesigned to fit the same operating potential into a smaller space, but if the railway can be fitted into the scenery rather than odd bits of scenery plonked into odd gaps, then it is possible to create a scenic whole in which the railway can actually come to life. My personal preference is to keep the actual railway area (ie, inside the railway fence) down to about 30 per cent of the area available. This has two desirable effects. The first is that with less track and fewer trains there is a lot less maintenance to contend with, and therefore more time for the joys of creating, and secondly, the fewer trains and the more pretty cottages etc, the more interesting wives, mother-in-laws and the non-cognoscenti find it. Perhaps a venture into the more unusual prototypes, where scratch building is essential, would allow a smaller model to capture the interest of the operator or viewer as much as a large model with trains dashing hither and thither to no particular purpose. It is however for you to decide — it's your railway.

So if you have decided on a scenic model, how does one actually start fitting what you want into the space you have available? Well firstly you decide on the part of the countryside you wish to model and upon what the terrain is like. Here it is as well to remember that height can often make up for lack of width in a model — bearing in mind that we look at models from the side, not the top as in plans — and that cottages often look cosiest set in a valley with hills behind and around them (Milton Abbas in Dorset is a classic example). With a mental picture of the landscape in mind the railway can then be planned to run through that terrain, just as it did in real life. Tunnels and curves become necessary rather than arbitrary. Engineering works such as tunnels, viaducts and embankments have to be placed where the track bed dictates. Rivers run at the bottom of valleys, canals perhaps partway up the side following a contour line. The railway may have to cross these, so arrange the railway so that you have footings for your bridges and access for passengers to your stations. Draw a large scale sketch of the area around your imaginary setting to decide where roads, tracks and lanes would go, put these on your model with a purpose and your railway will begin to serve a community. Later on, details of lorry or cart loads coming to or from your station can emphasize this as well as suggest the need for greater traffic than is immediately apparent from the scene you have modelled. Once you have introduced hills and valleys, viaducts and embankments, the term 'baseboard' becomes irrelevant. One simply needs a framework to hold up the track and scenery, whatever its level. In fact, having got rid of straight edges in a vertical sense there is no reason not to get rid of the straight edge at the edges of the baseboard as well. It is true that most railways are built against walls for some or all of the length, and that walls have a habit of being pretty straight things, but as walls are at the back of the layout from the onlookers point of view, they may usefully be straight, but they don't have to look it.

The horizon is the line beyond which you cannot see from any given point. If you have a headland or a cliff face, and you are standing at the bottom, then you cannot see what is on the top, so model your hill or cliff at a good height and roll the landscape backwards off the top adding a few large items such as trees or buildings to give scale. Looking down a valley it is often possible to see miles, so if your railway crosses a valley, taper the hills increasingly together in a parabolic shape, flattening them out as they reach the backscene and form a horizon again by rolling the scenery

The windmill, developed from a wooden kit, and its accompanying ramshackle sheds on the layout of the National Model Museum. The traction engine was converted from a showman's engine bought in the local toyshop. With a scene like this 'impressionist' describes the approach admirably. Save the exacting detail for the foreground where you can see it. (A. J. McMillan).

'You can't see the wood for the trees'. A few dozen varied specimens grouped thickly together create a delightful effect, and are all too seldom seen. None of these trees are brilliant examples of the modelmaker's art but the great variety of size, shape, texture, flow, and although you can't see it here, colour, all help to create the illusion of woods and forestry. (A. J. McMillan).

back out of sight. Then use perspective modelling, as in dioramas, to fit lots of ever smaller models as you work up the valley, details of which become less and less distinct along with the colouring, as they regress into the distance.

Fields and trees are most helpful in this direction and can also be arranged to join together hills and valleys that may only be three or four feet away in real life but have been modelled to look a mile or two apart. Study of the backgrounds in the accompanying photographs will, I hope, show what I mean. Produce each scenic section one chunk at a time adding the focal point and the visual barriers — dark woods, cliffs etc. It will probably take several attempts to produce a working drawing, but just think of the amount of work that goes into a model railway, whether it is on the flat or up and down the hills, and you will agree I am sure that time spent planning the setting to its best effect will pay dividends later. Do put on contour lines in actual inches height from the bottom of the model and do not forget, if the lowest part if the model is track, to leave room for wiring and point motors underneath! I think I will just go and have lunch while you work out your map. And dinner, supper, build the odd railway or two . .

If you now have a contoured plan on paper, it is time to recreate it in three dimensions. This is the time when all your planning begins to take shape, rapidly. So rapidly in fact that a sense of scale will quickly show up any mistakes or omissions, and a mistake now will be obvious forever, so work slowly. To make scenery this way you will need several sheets of 12mm shuttering ply, a jig saw (hire one for a fortnight if you don't want to buy one), a box a 2in × No 8 countersunk steel woodscrews (and a box of 1in × No 8), two 3-in-1 pilot drill, counter bore and counter sunk tools (1½in and 1in) and a large tube of good PVA wood glue

(Evostick Resin W is excellent). The layout should be divided into sections on the plan so that it can be assembled and if necessary moved. Each section should be no bigger than 8ft × 4ft. On huge layouts 8ft × 8ft is possible, or even 10ft × 10ft if using the larger specialist sheets, but how are you going to get to the middle to model the scenery? An 8ft × 4ft section is quite difficult enough to handle on its own but when placed on a couple of trestles at least one can reach the scenery from both sides!

Typical construction goes like this. Mark your drawing off at 18in intervals as a square grid. Draw vertical lines 18in apart across your sheet of 8 × 4 and mark the various heights taken from the drawing at 18in centres. Use 6in centres where the contours run close together or some feature on the skyline such as a castle demands an accurate shape. Using an artistic sweep of the hand, join the marks to give a cutting line and saw the section out, allowing the saw to sit about 45 degrees so that the scenery may be rolled over out of sight. Taking measurements at 90 degrees to the backscene, mark out in a similar way the various contours of the grid panels at 18in centres across the drawing. Taking the centre lines of any tracks crossing these contours, mark a road bed 3in wide for an embankment and 4in wide for a cutting, but remember to measure across the plane of the track. If the track crosses the former at 45 degrees, for example at a corner, then the flat bed of the track may be six or seven inches wide, for an acute angle even wider. If track on an embankment or in an earth cutting crosses a former at right angles, it will be an easy matter to project the angles of the earthworks up or down the level of the surrounding countryside but angled crossings will take a bit of working out. Earthworks are usually less than 45 degrees, sometimes if very loose materials are used or if a cutting is prone to slipping, as little as 30 degrees. This tends to make such features very noticeable and extravagant in the area they take up, but bridges and viaducts can help, as can rock cuttings in the right area.

The important point is that the landscape must continue at the same angle either side of any cutting or embankment, so as to give the impression that the landscape was there first. This is without doubt the foremost rule of successful landscaping and often a few inches here and there makes all the difference between convincing topography and 'toy hills'. Remember at a later stage that the railways bought all the land they needed, not just the track-bed, so put your fences back an inch or two from the edge of the earthworks. Sometimes even a single track running through flat countryside had its boundary fence thirty or forty feet back from the tracks. Look at a photo album for reference. Cut the contour out with the jig saw and check the height at the back with the back contour. The sections can now be screwed and glued together. Holding the cross contour in its place against the back contour, run a pencil down each side and remove. Taking a point in the dead centre of these two lines drill a few pilot holes, at least two and preferably three, into the back scene and on larger pieces every 8-10 inches. Running a line of glue along the edge of the cross contour, hold it in place against the back contour and using the pilot holes as a guide, drill a fixing hole with the 1½ in long 3-in-1 drill. Screw in through the back board into the end grain of the cross board with a 2in No 8 screw, ensuring that the bottom edges are level. Drill and fit the rest of the screws. Continue marking, cutting and fitting the rest of the contours until you end up with a backbone and ribs. When cutting the end pieces where a joint is made with another section, cut the two out together to ensure that they fit exactly. 'Nearly' is not good enough at these joints, or unsightly ridges will ruin the effect of the scenery, and your trains will fall off! The track bed is made of long thin off-cuts of the ply. These are never exactly the same height as the surrounding countryside. Even on a dead flat marshy landscape the railway would be on a two or three foot high embankment to allow for drainage. Cut your trackbeds 3 in wide for a single track (5 in for double) across the top of embankments and angle the cut outwards. Those who are really keen can actually go and measure the width of the embankment top, but look out for trains, they make a nasty mess of the strongest steep tape! Tracks beds for cuttings should be 6 in and 8 in wide to allow not only for a track bed, or two, but to give an inch or so for attaching the scenery to! When all the trackbeds are glued and screwed in place with the 1in screws the structure will become rigid. Finally procure a sheet of 6mm ply and fit a contour board along the front of the layout. There are many different ways of adding the base of the scenery to the contours, but my preference is for half inch chicken wire stapled to the timber with a staple gun, remembering to fold and crease in the shapes of your rivers, ditches, roads, embankments etc. Do not be afraid to cut or fold the mesh where necessary, securing with a few twists of tinned copper wire. Plaster bandage can be laid over this and voila! the model has taken shape! Before going any further remember that if you do not like any of it, now is the time to change it while it is still merely timber, mesh and plaster, so get out the plans, get the imagination going and make sure the roads are wide enough, the hills not too steep and that your favourite cottage — and its garden — will fit in the space you have left for it. There are of course a thousand and one minor problems to be encountered on the way, but if you can enjoy solving them that's half the fun!

A planning model

Michael Andress

Most railway modellers when constructing a layout, work from a scale plan. Often, to suit the size of paper easily available, or for convenience in handling the plan, this is to a relatively small scale. Even if drawn out to a larger size it is really quite difficult to envisage just what the completed three dimensional layout will look like by merely studying this plan.

A technique which is rarely employed by railway modellers but which can be of great value is the construction of a model of the proposed layout. Architects often make models of their designs prior to actual building construction. They are well aware that their clients will find it much easier to visualise the completed project from a model. In addition, the architects themselves, familiar though they are with interpreting plans often find it helpful to see the spatial relationships in a three dimensional representation so that minor modifications can be made to achieve the best possible final result. Such architectural models are also very helpful in planning the landscaping around the buildings. In the same way a model of your planned layout can give you a

much better idea of the visual effect which will result.

A study of the track plan will usually be effective in checking out the operational features such as choice of routings, siding placement and capacity, and so on. However, design errors and faults, particularly of a visual character may only be evident as the layout is built unless a model is constructed first. The three dimensional representation is especially useful in checking the arrangement of tracks on different levels and their relationships where they run close to or cross each other.

However, it is perhaps with the scenic planning for a layout that the model is most valuable. There is always a danger that in planning, the scenic setting will take second place to solving the problems of fitting in a track plan which will be interesting to operate. Even when the modeller does endeavour to consider the scenic effect during the planning stages it is difficult to visualise the overall appearance from a plan. A model, even a very simple one, will show this much more clearly and will enable the modeller to recognise

A typical 1:100 scale architectural planning and display model of a proposed development of two blocks of flats with garages. The three dimensional model makes it much easier to visualise the finished appearance of the buildings with their rather complex roof shapes and the overall effect of the landscaping than a study of two dimensional drawings. Materials employed in construction are typical of those used by railway modellers for structure and scenery modelling.

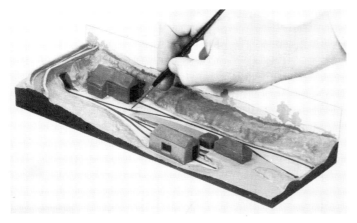

Dave Rowe made this neat planning model of a small branchline terminus using Peco texture modelling compound. The miniature gives an excellent idea of the appearance of the completed scene and enables any alterations desired to be made before construction of the station is begun.

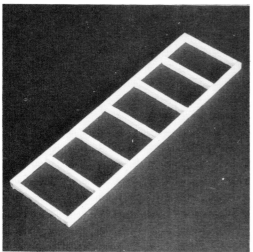

Stages in construction of a miniature planning model for a section of a layout. In this case baseboard construction was also represented to allow the modeller to check that the intended method would be suitable.

 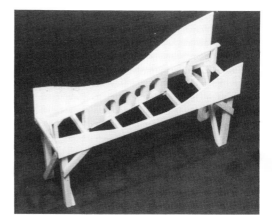

faults and problem areas. New arrangements can then be tried out on the model until the optimum visual effect and realism is achieved.

The time and effort required to build a planning model is small compared with the time, work and cost which can be involved if changes are needed at a late stage of actual construction. Indeed such changes may even be impossible by then without complete rebuilding so that the modeller may have to settle for a result which is not really as good as it could have been.

The model can be very simple, even crude, provided the dimensions are accurately scaled. Alternatively you may like to build quite a highly detailed and well finished miniature replica. The construction can be an interesting mini-project in itself and the completed 'model of a model' can

later be displayed beside your layout. If other members of the family have doubts about granting you right of way for a layout you may find that a nicely finished model showing just how neat and attractive the completed layout will be will help to persuade them in your favour. If the layout will have to be accommodated in the lounge a neat finish is essential. A very satisfactory method is to build the layout into a unit of furniture matching other items in the room. Again a preliminary model will help in the designing of a suitable housing.

A scale of 1in to 1ft is a useful one to choose as the model will be large enough for convenient visualisation but sufficiently small to be easy and quick to build. A simple method is to draw out the plan to this scale on a sheet of white card. Strips of

The completed planning model showing the viaduct and its setting. If desired other types of bridge and modifications in the landscaping can be tried out on this model to achieve the best possible effect. The bushes are tiny pieces of coloured foam scenic material.

card supported by small blocks of balsa are added to represent the elevated tracks. Alternatively if you also wish to check on the design of baseboard construction you can build this up using balsa or pine strip wood for the framework and risers and card strips for the track bed.

Any of the usual methods of scenery modelling can be employed, though on a smaller scale. However if you use Plasticine to model the contours of the landscape you can make alterations easily until you are satisfied with the appearance. If you wish you can then colour the model using ordinary model paints. Small blobs of green Plasticine will represent trees and hedges. Buildings can be simply small blocks of wood or can be modelled in rather more detail and painted

to give a realistic appearance. You can try the structures in various positions and groupings to achieve the best effect. In the same way, where a bridge is needed you can make simple models of different types and sizes of structure to see which will fit the situation best.

If you are planning a layout I would suggest that you consider making a preliminary model. It will assist you with all aspects of designing your layout but can be particularly helpful on the scenic side. Such a model will enable you to avoid many design faults and will make planning decisions much easier. The accompanying photographs show two examples of models built for planning sections of layouts.

Lee-on-the-Solent

Colin Hayward

Given our island situation, a railway running beside the sea is a fairly common occurrence. A railway terminus fifty feet from the beach, and almost level with it, is, however, something of a rarity. Many seaside towns, although welcoming the coming of the railway, banished it to the outskirts of the town. Prospective pleasure seekers had a long trek from the station to the beach, Bournemouth immediately springs to mind, and I'm sure that day-trippers, at any rate, might have had second thoughts about coming again, at least until bus services improved! One resort where absolutely no trekking whatsoever was required was Lee-on-the-Solent.

Lee-on-the-Solent, although many have never heard of it, let alone know that it once had a railway, was a bold town planning attempt of the late 1800s. Here was a watering place, its promoters hoped, with everything going for it. A splendid beach, a pleasant climate, superb sea views to the Isle of Wight, the sheltered waters of the Solent for boating and, of course, it was much nearer to London than Bournemouth, which was obviously the place to model it on.

Having purchased land, the Robinson family had a road system laid out to very generous proportions and proceeded to sell off building plots. A pier was opened in 1888 and regular steamboat services to Southsea and the Isle of Wight commenced, but any resort worth its salt at that time had to have a railway. The original plans for the resort had included a linear park area some 200 ft wide between the Marine Parade and the beach. This was fortuitous since it afforded an unobstructed route to bring the new railway right to the centre of things. Hence the terminus adjoining the beach.

This, then, I hope, sets the scene for my model. Having researched the whole history of the place in detail I was interested in somehow conveying the atmosphere of a Victorian/Edwardian seaside resort. The railway was obviously to be the focal point, with the red brick station building and its neighbouring structures providing a firm anchor, but there is more to it than that. After much consideration I decided that it was the very 'spaciousness' of the whole seafront scene which gave the place its atmosphere, and this was to be the all-important feature of the model. Here was to be a seafront with a railway, and not a railway by the sea. Think about it — there is an essential difference in emphasis.

This approach meant that I was going to have some fairly wide baseboards, since I wished to

Fig 1 Baseboards.

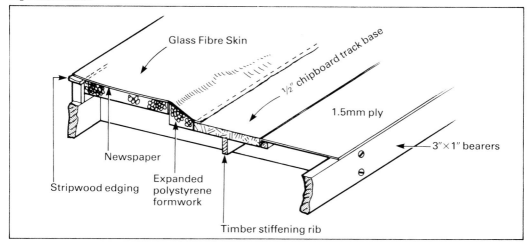

Glass Fibre Skin

½" chipboard track base

1.5mm ply

3"×1" bearers

Newspaper

Stripwood edging

Expanded polystyrene formwork

Timber stiffening rib

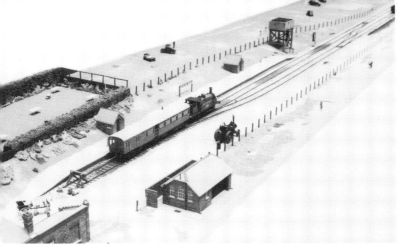

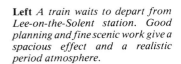

Left A train waits to depart from Lee-on-the-Solent station. Good planning and fine scenic work give a spacious effect and a realistic period atmosphere.

Two views of the station building, in the foreground, and the restaurant, behind. These scratchbuilt models are accurate replicas of the original buildings. The standard of modelling is very high; note particularly the realistic chimneys and other roof details.

portray, as near to scale as possible, the whole area between the Marine Parade and the beach. In 4mm scale this worked out at a little over two feet wide. I settled for rounding this down to two feet exactly. The layout was designed with exhibition in mind and I figured that anything wider would be just too unwieldy to move around easily. The length of the seafront area to be modelled broke down conveniently into three four-foot lengths with joints free from any pointwork. Apart from the sheer bulk when moving 4ft × 2ft sections around, the framing required meant that they could become very heavy once scenery was added. It was therefore essential to look at strong but lightweight materials.

The main baseboard frames were made from 3in × 1in planed timber, each frame having a centre cross-piece of the same size. Track bases of ½in chipboard were glued and screwed across the framing which immediately instilled a certain amount of rigidity, and the track bases were stiffened up with thin timber ribs to prevent sagging between supports (see Fig 1). At this stage each baseboard was clamped to its neighbour in turn, and holes were drilled right through both side members for fixing bolts. Ensure that the chipboard track bases align exactly before clamping and drilling — it's easy enough to pack out a bit of landscaping to match the next board but if your tracks don't meet each other perfectly you've got problems!

Track is laid next and it is essential that this is completely carried out and everything runs perfectly before attempting any scenery. The track in my case is 18.83mm gauge using 'Protofour' ply sleepers with bullhead rail soldered to rivets. Track was laid right across baseboard joints and glued down to a cork underlay. I use white glue to stick down the track sections, and pour ballast around it at the same time. Surplus ballast is carefully tipped off for re-use once the glue has dried and the rails bridging

Closer views of the platform area. The wattle fencing along the railway side of the garden and the railway boundary fences are well shown in these pictures. The traction engine is a repainted Matchbox 'Yesteryear' model with extra detailing.

the baseboard joints have been carefully cut through with a razor saw. Whilst the glue is drying the track sections should be heavily weighted down to ensure a level running surface.

Once the track is down, scenic work can start in earnest. I first fit all the 'hard' surfaces — roads, promenade, station plaform, etc. These were all put in as a thin 'skin' of 1.5mm marine ply. Ply is thin but strong, and can be easily curved over light wooden formers which will stiffen it up. Before finishing the grain should be disguised with filler or stopping. The surface is then sanded down smooth and the desired treatment added. To convey the general feel of a seaside area, a large part of my model was treated with a sandy colour-ed emulsion paint, and sand sprinkled on while wet. This gives a texture which can be given a second coat of emulsion when dry. To add high-lights and vary the overall sameness of the emulsion colour, the textured surface is worked up with an almost dry brush of oil-based paint to give the effect of gravel, wheel marks, coal stains, etc. The gravelled yard at Lee-on-the-Solent led direct to the station platform which was similarly gravelled. Study of old photographs indicates that the gravelled platform was very common before the widespread adoption of tarmacadam

surfacing, yet it is not too often modelled. The platform edge, somewhat unusually, was of mass concrete rather than brick — indeed this was standard construction on all the original halts on the line. I represented the concrete with a thin ply wall, topped with cardboard capping. The curve between the wall and the capping was simulated with a fillet of woodworkers' stopping. The whole thing was painted with an overall matt colour of matured concrete, and then streaked with weather marks. The edge was painted white to simulate whitewash, not forgetting splashes down the front face! Most of the 'hard' surfacing is applied direct to the framing. The only part to be built up is at the level crossing. The thin ply is swept up here to rest on the sleepers, with the edge hard up against the rail. Slight packing or filing should ensure that it does not actually come above rail level. The shoulders of the road were sloped down with filler to a sub-base which should extend about an inch either side of the road proper to form a bearing for the grassed areas of the scenery.

Next came the grassed areas. I had to hand a quantity of expanded polystyrene packing material about 1in thick. As the ground is gently undulating, I figured this could be used as a base.

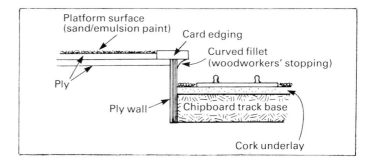

Fig 2 Platform construction.

Carefully cut to size it can be pushed into place between wooden (ply) formers. Expanded polystyrene on its own is liable to damage easily, as can often be seen on exhibition model railway layouts, so that white scars show through. I therefore gave it a tough outer skin of glass fibre reinforced resin. As the resin reacts with expanded polystyrene and dissolves it there has to be an intermediate layer. The polystyrene was covered with strips of newspaper pasted on with wallpaper paste. Use fairly small strips and overlap them to prevent the resin from leaking through later. When the paper is thoroughly dry, apply a coat of resin with an old brush, and then overlay with a glass fibre mat (these materials can be obtained at car accessory shops). Carefully dab more resin on to the mat and expel all air bubbles. This can be a little tricky at first as the glass fibre has a tendency to lift up on the sticky brush. Tackle about a square foot at a time. Use a pair of polythene disposable gloves or you'll probably end up with resin on your hands, and it can cause skin irritations. When the resin had set, the whole grassed area was given a uniform coat of matt green paint. For texturing I am now firmly converted to Woodland Scenics materials. I mix the colours and sprinkle on to slightly diluted white glue. Patches of light 'burnt grass' were worked in, since the underlying gravelly soil would have been poor and prone to dry out during the summer months. In contrast to the worn, tired appearance of the open public grassed areas the garden was to have a neat well-tended look. A richer green scenic material was used, care being taken to give the lawn tidy edges. The surrounding flower beds were painted dark brown, with sand sprinkled on whilst wet.

Plants are a mixture of items. Tufts of sisal string can be stuck end-on into a blob of white glue. When painted green with a generous blob of orange/red paint at the end of some of the fibres

you have a good representation of 'red-hot pokers'. Stained with a diluted wash of red-brown, sisal string can simulate ornamental shrubs such as dog-wood. With a tuft of Woodland Scenics' foliage planted on top, a thick bush, and so on. Again, low-lying border plants can be formed of Woodland Scenics with dabs of coloured paint for flowers. I found some 12in to the foot clematis seeds lying in my garden and these were stuck in to give an impression of more delicate foliage.

The hedges appear to have been fairly dense in all the photographs I could find. To give them a bit of body I took a piece of ½in thick balsa and hacked rough, irregular V-shaped nicks into it (see sketch). The whole block was painted a very dark green, almost black, and then a thin covering of the Woodland Scenics foliage was stuck onto the sides, top and ends, allowing the dark green paint to show through in places. The hedge nearest to the station platform grew beside a woven wattle fence. Boggling at the prospect of weaving a dozen or so fencing panels out of thin wire, I discovered to my great relief that Merit Accessories produce a nice little pack of this type of fencing. If you cut off the lugs at the bottom, and paint them up, they look most convincing. The fence panels were stuck to the face of the hedge, and then glued into place. A similar fence ran along the back of the garden, but with a wooden trellis arrangement to (presumably) support rambler roses. To model this, stripwood uprights and horizontals were added to the Merit panels.

The railway boundary fence is Ratio pointed top posts. I discarded the plastic 'wire' as being too thick. I had found, in one of my local shops, rolls of tungsten wire — 100 yards or so for 50p. The scale diameter is about ¼in, so I decided to try this. In the event, it was not entirely satisfactory. Since tungsten is very smooth, I had difficulty in fixing the wire to the plastic posts without leaving an untidy blob of glue at each fixing. Having driven myself barmy the night before the layout went on show, I decided to leave the strands on the other fencing out altogether. On reflection, it probably looks better! I feel that the tungsten wire could be used with the type of posts where the wire actually passes through the body of each post. The farm-type gates at the level crossing are Peco.

When first put on show, the model had no beach or sea, though this was part of the original plan. Subsequently a set of 'screw-on' front panels has been made. This can probably be most easily explained by reference to the accompanying drawing. A piece of 2in × ½in timber has

Fig 3 Hedges.

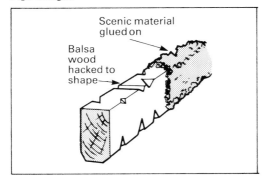

Scenic material glued on

Balsa wood hacked to shape

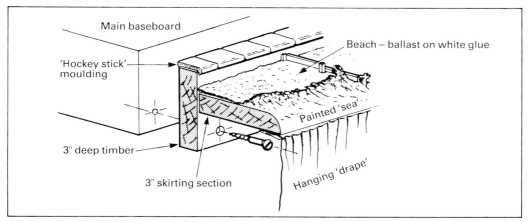

Main baseboard

'Hockey stick' moulding

Beach – ballast on white glue

3" deep timber

Painted 'sea'

3" skirting section

Hanging 'drape'

Above *Fig 4* Screw-on beach sections.

Right *A further view of the station and restaurant with the garden complete with tables and wheelbarrow. Modelling of the grass, plants and hedges is described in the text.*

been fixed at right angles to a piece of 3in skirting moulding. The top of the first piece of timber has been capped with a 'hockey-stick' section moulding to represent the sea wall. This was scored to simulate the joints in the stone slabs, filled with stopping, and painted a brownish grey stone colour. The skirting section was painted the same sandy colour as the roadways before being coated thickly with white glue, and sprinkled liberally with brownish ballast to form a beach. Some of the skirting is left as sea — represented with bluish-green and white paint. This looked a bit dead, so I got out an old tub of textured ceiling paint which I had in the garage. It had almost all gone hard with age but sufficient remained for me to indulge in some 'artistic effects' in the form of waves breaking on the shore. The textured paint has enough body to make quite convincing breakers. If you want bigger waves, leave it to dry off for a day, and then build on what is already there. Breakwaters were formed of stripwood. These beach sections can be screwed to the front of the

main baseboard sections, and the whole effect is finished off with a greenish-blue fabric drape suspended from the 'bull-nose' edge of the skirting section.

Although this article is primarily concerned with scenics, a word or two about the buildings will probably not go amiss since they are an essential part of the sea-front scene. All the buildings lift out for storage and transport, holes either being left whilst constructing the scenery or cut out subsequently. I favour styrene sheet for building since it gives a good strong structure and, provided thick enough sheet is used and sufficient internal bracing applied, it does not distort. I believe I used 60 thou thick sheet for the larger buildings. Window apertures etc, are probably most easily cut out using a piercing saw, the final shaping up being carried out with a file. I was particularly fortunate in that the Builder Plus red brick paper is a perfect representation of the local red brick. This was applied to the styrene by soaking with solvent. Keep your windows open while you're doing this! At first I produced tiled roofs by scribing the plastic sheet, but I later discovered an embossed sheet which gave a good impression of roof tiles. The only major building without brick facing was the boat house. Unfortunately this no longer exists, but photographs showed it to have had a pebble dash finish with brick quoins. Again, paint liberally sprinkled with sand was used, this time to simulate pebble dash. The roof covering was a bit indistinct in the photographs, but could well have been diamond-pattern asbestos slates, represented by scoring the styrene sheet diagonally and painting pale grey. A little yellow lichen is not out of place on this type of roof covering.

Window frames etc, are carefully cut out from thin styrene sheet. It's more tedious than ruling white lines on clear plastic but I think the finished result is worth it. Finials and other little details are carved up from different thicknesses of styrene. The decorative ridge tiles on the restaurant build-ing and the platform shelters are made by drilling a row of equally spaced holes in a strip of plastic and then cutting carefully right through the middle to leave a series of scallops.

Having completed the scene, the period was established with the help of figures and vehicles. The John Piper series of 1920s figures (unfortun-ately, I believe, no longer available), if carefully painted, really look the part. Road vehicles are a Matchbox Yesteryear traction engine (made pre-sentable by dousing in paint stripper, repainting and detailing), some Slaters horse-drawn vehicl-es, and some small plastic car kits of Spanish manufacture (being HO scale I keep them towards the back of the scene). I recently saw the new Yesteryear 'Old Bill' open top bus, and I fancy that with a bit of emerald and white paint it will pass muster as one of the early Gosport 'Provincial' fleet parked in the station yard.

So there we have it. . . an Edwardian holiday resort lives again!

Ipsley Circle – 'Coombe Mellin' river scene

David Simmonite

The enjoyment of model railways can extend far beyond just laying track and operating trains. For us, the 'Ipsley Circle', it enters the realms of constructing buildings, scenery and other ancillary items often requiring the development of other skills. At exhibitions, layouts which attract our attention are those on which a great deal of time and effort has been expended to create a whole railway scene rather than just a good operating network. This was our approach when planning and later constructing 'Coombe Mellin'.

A search through many books finally unearthed an early photograph of a swing bridge at Turnchapel, Plymouth, where the old London & South Western line crossed the river estuary. This interesting bridge consisted of three spans, two fixed and one swinging, which we felt would both harmonize with the rest of the layout and be a challenge to build. Choosing an actual location to model is often easier than trying to create an imaginary scene which can result in giving that contrived look.

Before work actually started a reasonably detailed drawing of the various elements of the bridge and its environs was prepared. Reference to the photographs showed the bridge to be in three sections, the outer spans of lattice design and the centre swinging span of plate girder design. Any thought of an operating swing bridge was eliminated at this stage as an exhibition layout has to be reliable—although this decision was taken with a tinge of regret. The main dimensions of the scene are shown on the plan and elevations, and these formed the basis of all subsequent constructional work.

The baseboard was 914mm long × 762mm wide with the complete bridge spanning 772mm. The baseboard side members were constructed from two thicknesses of 9mm ply glued and pinned together, the outside layer being 76mm deep and the inside layer 63.5mm deep. This allows for insertion of the 12.7mm thick chipboard panels. The ends were of similar construction except that the outside layer was 152mm deep giving approximately 62mm clearance between the bridge and water. As will be seen from the drawings, the outer and inner layers were not of the same

length, enabling the interlocking of the corner joints, themselves further strengthened with pieces of 51mm × 51mm timber glued and screwed through the sides and ends.

Before finally joining the sides and ends consideration was given to the method for accurately joining adjacent baseboards, particularly important if the layout is portable. We used brass dowels to align the boards and 6mm diameter bolts to hold them together. By clamping the ends of adjacent boards they can be drilled as a pair, ensuring accurate alignment when the dowels are inserted and good trackwork over the joints. Side and end members can then be glued and pinned together to form the frame. Two pieces of 12.7mm (½in) chipboard were glued into the frame at either end and the river gap between filled with another piece set below the end pieces to provide depth to the river. Cross bracing of the frame was added, together with the legs which fold up underneath for storage purposes. The next addition was the stone abutments to the bridge made from blocks of fine grained wood, glued in position after the stone finish had been carved into the surface. The abutments support the bridge and provide a good

Fig 1 Baseboard details.

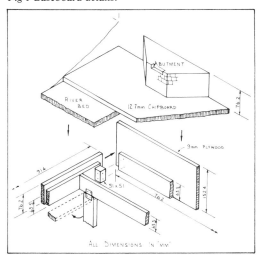

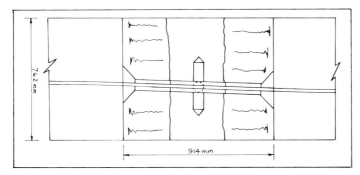

Left *Fig 2* Plan of baseboard.

Below *A goods train rumbles slowly across the swing bridge. The river has a realistic sparkle in this backlit view.*

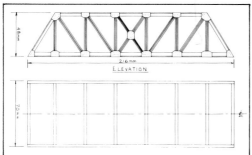

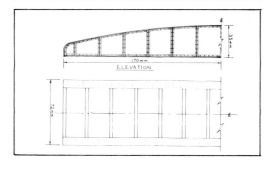

foundation for rigidly fixing the track in the most vulnerable area, the baseboard joint.

Finally, the baseboard and adjacent boards were erected, bolted together and carefully levelled so that the joints could be planed to produce a smooth even surface for the 3mm cork trackbed. An important point, often ignored, is the addition of strips of 12mm × 3mm deep hardwood on the edges of the baseboard to which the sleepers are glued for track stability.

The construction of the outside spans was made easier by the purchase of two Airfix lattice bridge kits, these providing the four main trusses. Two of these were glued to the outside edges of a piece of 60 thou plastic card 216mm long × 70mm wide and cross girders of 'I' section Plastruct added between them at the panel points. Whilst the glue is setting support the side frames in a vertical position as there is a tendency for them to lean inwards. Repeat for the second span.

Above left *Fig 3* Elevation and plan of the end spans.
Left *Fig 4* Elevation and plan of the swinging span.

The plate girder swinging span had to be scratch built as there was nothing available commercially. The lower flange was cut from 20 thou plastic card and and laid down on a smooth, flat surface. A web of 40 thou material was glued along the centre line of the flange forming an inverted 'T' section. The top flange of 20 thou material with rivet detail added was glued in position on the web, the ends being glued down to meet the lower flange. Web stiffeners were added at intervals along the girder with the rivetted angle section being represented by strips of plastic card. Repeat for the second girder. To finish the swinging span the two girders were glued to the outside edges of a piece of plastic card 340mm long × 72mm wide and 'I' section cross beams added as for the outside spans.

Reference to the original photograph showed the swinging span to be resting on a substantial column and collar and the outer spans supported by twin smaller columns suitably cross braced. On the model the central pier was made from 37mm diameter plastic tube and the collar from various plastic sections. The outer piers were of 19mm diameter dowel with cross bracing from 'L' section plastic. Great care was exercised when making the piers to ensure they were to the correct height, allowing for the bridge construction depth, to ensure a level track right across the baseboard. At this stage all the various bridge sections were painted a medium grey.

On the bridge the track was laid on baulk timber, ideal in modelling terms as it provides a continuous track bed. Two pieces of lime 4mm thick × 8mm wide × 772mm long were pinned, parallel to one another 10.90mm apart, on a smooth, flat surface and 4mm square cross bracing glued at intervals between them. Cast white metal chairs were added to the baulks with instant glue and when dry metre lengths of bullhead threaded through the chairs leaving a 114mm overlap at each end to which sleepers were soldered as in standard S4/P4 constructional methods.

Next came the erection of the piers which, having been accurately located, were held rigidly in the vertical position while the glue set. Before adding the bridge sections the river banks, whose gentle slopes feathered out on the river bed near the outer piers, needed to be built up using Modroc supported by rolled up newspaper and cardboard.

The timber protection to the centre pier was made in-situ from 5mm square timber and lengths of crossing sleepers. It does not matter if it ends up slightly misaligned as this gives the feeling the protection has been there for years and suffered many knocks and bangs from passing boats. In fact, this item owes some of its charm to the little child who grabbed a handful at one exhibition. The banks and river bed can now be painted the slimy green colour so often found in tidal waters and the protection a weathered timber colour.

The river itself was made from clear casting resin which produced a good representation of water, but this takes some time to fully set. Be sure to mix and pour the resin in a well ventilated area, preferably outside, because the fumes are exceedingly unpleasant and hang around for many days. The resin was poured in thin layers gradually building up a reasonable depth, in this case about 18mm, and the top surface painted with a murky green emulsion. It had been intended to cover this with a final thin layer of resin. However, in drying, the emulsion seemingly reacted with the hardened resin below and produced ripples very reminisent of flowing water; the final coat was never added. It just goes to show, sometimes apparent problems have happy endings, although we could not guarantee a similar exercise would produce similar results. In fact had the final layer been added the surface

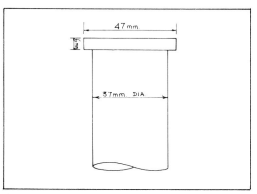

Above *Fig 5* Central Pier.
Below *Fig 6* Outer Pier.

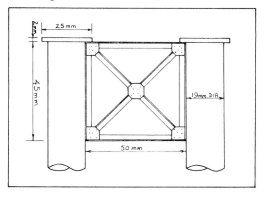

Right and below *Two further views of the bridge showing the very neat modelling of the bridge and its supports. The small open boats add interest to the realistically modelled river banks. Note the boat yard near the 'whistle' sign on the far side of the river. A boat under construction is just visible inside the building and the boat yard has a launching ramp leading down into the river.*

would have had to be plucked as it hardened to produce the ripple effect, a time consuming job.

The baseboard and two adjacent boards were again erected and carefully levelled and the three bridge spans fixed in position. The previously constructed track on its timber baulks was glued in position across the bridge with the sleepered ends, which overlap the baseboard joints, suitably ballasted and left to dry. After this the track at the baseboard joint was cut using a carborundum wheel ensuring good alignment of the track and a smooth passage of trains from one baseboard to another. The final stage was the addition of the timber walkway across the bridge and provision of vegetation, trees, etc.

Having completed the river and bridge we all agreed the scene lacked activity and there was a need for a boat. Therefore, in the usual democratic way, I was volunteered the task. As the baseboard is only 2ft 6in wide it was essential to choose a boat not so big as to overpower the scene, or so small that it might just as well not be there. A visit to my local library produced an excellent book, *The Construction of Model Open Boats* by Ewart C. Freeston, which apart from describing some of the different types of open boats, included sufficient information for a reasonable model to be made. I had decided prior to finding the book that the boat eventually

chosen to model would involve only a modest amount of work as my main interest was in creating a railway scene. From the book I found the two-masted coble to be of good size being approximately 120mm × 27mm × 10mm in 4mm scale. Although geographically such a boat would not have been found in the supposed location of our railway, this was obviously another case of modelling licence being used to create a scene pleasing to the eye.

The general features of the coble developed from the need to launch boats from the shore in all types of weather in areas with few harbours. Thus the coble has a sharp bow, flat body and a long rudder which acts as an extra keel. Another characteristic was the small number of full width planks, each overlapping the one below to form the clinker built hull. My modelling techniques were chosen to produce a reasonable model without resorting to too much detail. They are based on those used many years ago in my model aircraft days, which only goes to show that techniques developed in one area of modelling can be used in another. No doubt many will recall laying out the plan of an aircraft wing on a flat surface and pinning the main struts in position, glueing the wing sections in place and gradually building up the whole structure. My method involved glueing the various cross sections upside down on a

The beautifully detailed coble was built from scratch; construction is described fully in the text. The smaller open boat in the background was built in a similar way.

plan, thus forming a rigid master around which the boat can be built.

The first stage in producing a boat is to obtain or draw a plan and sections of your choice. If drawing your own plans they do not have to be an engineering masterpiece as long as the boat lines are carefully reproduced. Each individual cross section, in this case six, was transferred to 1mm card, making allowances for the thickness of the planking. I found pricking through to be the best method of transferring points from the plan, but do ensure that all the important points are included, particularly the top of the boat side where the planking finishes. You will note that the cross sections have been extended to a datum line so that when cut out and glued upside down on the plan the resultant master mould gives the shape of the finished hull. Once the cross sections have been cut out, and before they are glued down onto the master, consideration must be given to the location of the planking. My model has seven full width planks and consideration of the hull shape will show those planks in the middle to be wider than at the bow and stern. Therefore, the girth at each cross section must be measured and each

half divided into seven by whatever method you find most convenient. With each cross section cut out and the position of the planks marked, they were glued upside down on the plan, previously fixed to a flat surface, such as a sheet of glass (see drawing).

For planking, filing card was used as it is thin but forms a suprisingly rigid hull when the model is complete. A word of warning, do not pull the planking too tightly around the master as this tends to create ridges where the planking passes over a cross section. You could equally well use thin wood veneer of the type used in marquetry which might give a better line to the finished hull. However, some trouble may be experienced in bending the veneer to the complex shape to be formed. Although strictly the coble does not have a full keel, for ease of construction I built up out of wood a half keel including bow and stern posts, which is held in position on the master by pins rather than glue. The reason for this will become apparent as the model progresses.

The planking is started at the keel, which is convenient and gives a straight edge for marking out. A straight line is drawn on a piece of filing

Many examples of the type of swing bridge described in this article can be seen with minor variations in style and detail. This bridge in Sweden has two fixed through truss girder spans but the swing section is a deck girder span instead of a plate girder. The bridge is also lower and has stone piers.

card and the positions of the cross sections drawn perpendicular to this line. With a pair of dividers measure from the master the width of the first plank at each section and the position where the plank meets the bow and stern. Transfer these measurements to the relevant perpendiculars on the card. You should now have a series of points which are connected together with a smooth curve giving you the first shaped plank. Continue for the remainder of the planks by marking out widths of each using the curved outside of the previous planks as your datum, increasing each plank width slightly to allow for the overlap of the clinker built hulls. Repeat using another piece of card for the other side of the hull.

The next step is tricky but, with a little care, a good result can be expected. Take the first plank and with a little thinned PVA glue position it against the keel, making sure no glue comes into contact with the master or you will not be able to separate the boat from the mould at a later stage. Do the same for the other side. Then continue, with the second planks overlapping the first by approximately ½ millimeter and so on until all seven have been added to both sides finishing at the top of the hull mark on the cross section. (Note that planking is added to either side alternately thus avoiding any distortion of the hull.) Allow time to dry thoroughly. Once dry the hull can be gently eased off the master and a little thinned glue is worked into the areas where the glue was omitted. You should now have a stable structure and the work from here on is mainly cosmetic, although obviously it does also add to the strength of the finished article.

The frames are spaced at approximately 10mm centres and can be represented by cutting ¾mm wide strips from 5 thou card. These are glued in position with the ends overlapping the gunwale and are trimmed off when the glue has set. The frames can be added as complete pieces, except those of the bow and stern of the boat where they will have to be added to each side separately. Following the trimming of the sections the gunwale can be added. As these were 2½in × 2½in timber I would suggest a change of material to 1mm ply which is very flexible and can easily be cut with a scalpel. Cut a piece of ply to a size which will overlap by, say, 10mm all round the boat and gently press down onto the top of the boat shell. Lightly draw round the outside of the shell, thus transferring the shape of the boat to the ply. Smooth out any irregularities in the pencil line and draw two new lines ½mm either side of the original line taking care to include the shaped ends at the bow and stern. You now have the gunwales marked out on the ply and all that remains is to carefully cut out the shape and glue onto the boat shell. The next step is adding the stringer, which is again cut from the ply and runs horizontally from bow to stern. At this stage I would suggest giving the whole boat a coating of 'patent knotting'; this contains shellac which seals the card, stiffens the structure and provides a base for the final painting. It also has a colour very representative of a yacht varnish finish. I left the inside of the boat unpainted, but should you wish to paint the interior also, now is the time to do it.

All that was left to complete the boat was the addition of seats, rudder, mast tabernacle, mast and rigging.

Modelling Rheinfalle Gorge

David and Mike Polglaze

'Die Bernhardinbahn' is an HO scale (3.5mm to the foot) metre gauge (HOm) layout based on a part of the Rhätische Bahn, or Rhaetian Railway, in Switzerland that was never actually built. The RhB is a metre gauge line that serves the largest canton in the Swiss Federation, Graubünden. The railway starts at Chur and serves such well known places as Klosters, Davos and St Moritz. Today the Rhaetian Railway network is very well known even as it is, but if the planners and builders had been able to develop the system as they intended the railway would have been much more extensive. One line was planned to run from Schuls to Landeck in Austria where it would have linked with the Österreichische Bundesbahnen (ÖBB—the Austrian Federal Railways). Another would have gone beyond St Moritz to Chiavenna in Italy, connecting with the Ferrovie dello Stato (FS — Italian State Railways). A third would have stayed within the Swiss borders running from Thusis to Bellizona via the St Bernhardin Pass.

We did seriously consider building a model based on the line to Landeck but because the Bernhardin route sounded more spectacular and of the three projected routes was the one which came closest to actually being built, it finally became our choice. The details of this route are well covered in John Marshall's book *Metre Gauge Railways in South and East Switzerland* published in 1974 by David & Charles. To anyone modelling Swiss narrow gauge this book is a must. We don't know if it is still in print but with the upsurge of interest as a result of the introduction of the Bemo and other models perhaps David & Charles might consider updating and reprinting it.

When we knew Bemo were going to introduce Rhaetian Railway models we imagined that many layouts based on the railway would appear. We felt we wanted something a bit different and so the village of Hinterrhein was selected. Quite why we chose Hinterrhein we can't remember but no doubt we were influenced by the fact that it would have been the last station before the Bernhardin Tunnel and that it was the summit of the northern ramp which would mean that there were no steep

The gorge disguises the curve leading to the hidden sidings and makes it appear necessary because of the terrain. Behind the bridge a waterfall plunges down the rock face to feed the river in the gorge far below.

After leaving the bridge the line runs along a ledge above the valley. The rock faces were cast from plaster as described in the text.

gradients on the model. One mistake we did make was to build the model some two years before we visited the village of Hinterrhein. When we eventually did go and look we found the prototype didn't follow the model! Never mind, that's one advantage of semi-freelance models!

The trouble with model railways is that they must be built in confined spaces and no matter how big or small a layout is, sooner or later the tracks reach the end of the baseboard and have to disappear behind the scenery to connect with the rest of the world, usually in the form of hidden sidings. Many ways have been devised to deal with the disappearance of the tracks and there is no doubt that the tunnel is by far the most popular means. Die Bernhardinbahn is no exception. At one end it runs into the 5 kilometre St Bernhardin Tunnel but at the other end we wanted something eye-catching to disguise the curve and to divert attention from the line's exit. Thus the Rheinfalle Gorge was planned and built. Anyone who has

travelled by train in Switzerland will know the sensation of coming out of a tunnel and suddenly finding themselves crossing a bridge high above a valley. This was the effect we wanted to achieve.

Any modeller, if he is honest, will admit to being influenced by others and we are no exception. Apart from falling under the spell of Switzerland, and who wouldn't, for the prototype, both railway and scenery, it is from across the Atlantic that our scenic modelling inspiration has come. Three Americans in particular have influenced our modelling. The late John Allen with his 'Gorre & Daphetid' layout, Dave Frary who models New England narrow gauge prototypes and Malcolm Furlow. We have read and re-read the writings of these experts and have employed many of the techniques they describe in our scenic work. Why go across the Atlantic for ideas you may ask. Look at pictures of some of the American layouts; there is no doubt that they are a long way ahead in scenic modelling. Also

This view from above the bridge gives a good impression of the depth of the gorge. There are many small details included in the gorge area; among them are two girls about to take a topless swim in the pool at the foot of the waterfall and just visible in this scene far below the bridge to the left of the river.

On a small wooden bridge across the river hikers pause to admire the view. Note the signpost on the right.

many of their layouts are based on mountainous country, which after all is what Switzerland is.

Having made up our minds to go 'Euro-American' as it were, we started on the layout. Before any construction work was done we drew up plans and made sketches to clarify just how we thought the finished model should look. We decided to construct open top baseboards with the track level about a foot above the base level giving plenty of room for scenery both above and below track level. The American author Dave Frary recommends splitting a layout up into separate 'theme scenes' each relatively complete in itself scenically but with something to lead the eye from one to another. This idea is explored a little further in our later article on modelling small scenes, but in the meantime we would merely mention that Rheinfalle Gorge was designed on this principle.

The baseboard for the gorge section measures 3ft by 2ft and the first stage was to mark out where the track would be sited and where the river and the gorge walls would be positioned. This was done with frequent reference to the sketch we had made previously. When we were satisfied with the marking out, the track supports were fitted and the trackbed laid, including the bridge section. The trackbed is Sundeala on 5 ply which gives a solid but quiet base for the track. Next the trackwork was laid using Peco Code 80 FB rail spiked to wooden sleepers. In fact at this stage we installed all the trackwork for the whole layout, wired it up and fully tested it before proceeding with the scenery. Once testing was satisfactorily completed the track in the area to be landscaped was covered using newspaper and masking tape so that none of the scenic materials got onto the track or track bed. At this stage no ballasting had been done.

The next job was to put in the scenic framework. First the gorge walls were erected using thick cardboard and bits of wood glued into the required places using the drawn lines as guides. A space was left for the tunnel mouth to be fitted

The footpath runs alongside the river on the floor of the gorge. Extensive use is made of Woodland Scenics materials for the grass and vegetation.

The impressive pine trees were hand built with trunks of balsa and Asparagus Fern for the branches.

later. The foundation for the ground above the gorge was also installed but that over the track was left loose so that the track is accessible for maintenance or in case of derailment of a train. At the same time as the gorge walls were fitted formers were also cut and fitted to give the steep slopes from above the tracks down to the baseboard edges. When building any layout, particularly a mountain line, remember that in the real world the scenery would be there first and the railway route cut through it later, and your scenic work should give the same impression. On our layout the line runs along a ledge after crossing the bridge in order to reach the station which is high above the valley floor.

Once all the formers had been installed and the glue had thoroughly dried out, the whole area was covered with a criss-cross pattern of material ready to take the plaster shell. We have used various items for this including strips of card and masking tape but our favourite is plasterers gauze. We now employ this gauze for all our scenery. The gauze was cut into strips and stuck down with white glue. When dry this forms quite

a strong base. Any trimming was carried out after it had dried out fully. Over any spaces between formers we pushed in balls of newspaper behind the gauze to give it shape. This was helped by spraying the gauze with water to soften it and make it easier to shape. The balls of paper were removed after the scenery shell was finished.

Now comes the mucky part. Making sure the track and also the river bed were well covered to protect them, the plaster was applied. The Americans call this 'hard shell scenery'. Unfortunately the products they use, identified by American trade names, do not appear to be available here and this has meant that we have had to find eqivalent British materials, which we realise are not quite the same as the ones 'over there'. For plaster we mostly use the pink plaster used on walls in houses, or at times plaster of paris. We buy the pink plaster in 4 kilogram bags at our local DIY shop. Prior to plastering we tear up paper towels into squares about 4 to 6in in size, using industrial grade rather than the kitchen roll type which is rather too flimsy. The plaster is mixed in a bowl to a creamy mix, not making up too much at once,

The farm houses above the gorge were built from Kibri kits with extra details. The figures are mainly from the Preiser range.

The small stacks of hay in the field were modelled with cotton wool wrapped around cocktail sticks and covered with yellow-green Noch electrostatic grass. At the left is the river above the gorge and the top of the waterfall.

and squares of the paper are dipped into the plaster, soaked and then laid on the gauze web, with each square overlapping the one before. We work from bottom to top. The whole area of the gorge section was done at the same time, taking two evenings to apply two layers.

Having completed the basic shell we faced the gorge walls with rock mouldings. This is a technique not much used in Britain whereas in the United States rock moulding has been around for many years and is a popular method for modelling rock faces. To make the moulds we bought a kit of latex moulding rubber, intended for children, from our local art and craft shop. We selected several suitable pieces of rock and lumps of coal, choosing ones of about hand size and with a good strata; coal tends to have an especially suitable pattern. To make a mould the rock is well washed to remove any loose bits and dirt. While still wet the first coat of latex is brushed on; the rock being wet helps the latex to run into all the little nooks and crannies. Altogether about seven layers are applied. After the first four we include a layer of small squares of gauze which helps to strengthen the mould. The final coat is a mixture of latex and very fine sawdust, usually supplied with the kit. We leave the mould for about 24 hours to dry and then peel it very carefully from the rock. Several moulds are made at the same time to provide variety.

To cast a rock we make a creamy mix of pink plaster and pour it into the pre-wetted mould. We use two different methods of rock moulding. One is to let the plaster dry out in the mould before removing it, a technique known as dry moulding. The alternative is to let the plaster semi-set only and place it onto a pre-wetted plaster base. This is wet moulding. Several moulds are used at the same time. We can usually tell when a mould is ready to come off; one good clue is that the

moulding gets warm as it dries out. Any gaps between mouldings are filled in with broken bits of dry mouldings stuck on with plaster used like cement. The tunnel mouth was fitted at this stage and secured by the rock mouldings around it.

Colouring the scene comes next. The American modeller Dave Frary has pointed out that in real life scenery everything takes on the colour of the soil in the particular area and if you look around at nature you will find that this is true. We started with an earth colour paint on all those areas which would be grassed. The Americans use latex paint but the nearest we have found is flat vinyl emulsion. Whether it is similar or not we don't know but it works very well. For the earth paint on Die Bernhardinbahn we used a colour called Catalan. This is a Crown Plus Two paint and we use the Matchpots. We water the paint down one to one with water and add a touch of white emulsion. Before applying the paint the plaster is given a good soaking with 'wet water' which is water with a few drops of washing up liquid. The detergent makes the water flow onto the plaster and wet it better. The paint is then brushed onto about 18in square or less at a time, depending on the terrain. We find it best to pre-wet the plaster as described above because otherwise the dry plaster draws the paint in so quickly it is difficult to get the surface covered. As soon as the paint is on it is covered with Woodlands Blended Turf scenic dressing. This is only the base but grassing is left until later while the rocks are dealt with.

Our rock plant is made up from a Crown Matchpot called Winter Mist which has a blue tint in it. This is watered down one to one and a touch of earth paint and a few drops of Rotring black drawing ink are also added. It is very much a case of trial and error and testing on bits of old plaster. When ready, the rocks are sprayed with 'wet water' and painted, the paint being worked into every nook and cranny. While still wet the rocks are sprayed with watered down Rotring black drawing ink, which is water soluble, with a couple of drops of detergent in it. This not only darkens the rocks but also runs into all the cracks accentuating them and enhancing the texture effect of the rock surface.

We crushed some rock castings with a hammer and scattered the pieces along the river bed and around the base of the waterfall. At this stage these rocks were not fixed down but left loose so that we could move them about until the scene looked right. At the same time some twigs and scale sized logs were positioned on the rocks. Eventually when we were satisfied that all was as we wanted it we stuck the whole lot down using a one to one mix of Resin W and water. Prior to pouring on the glue the whole area was sprayed with 'wet water' which helps to carry the glue around and between the rocks.

The next stage was to model the waterfall. To try to obtain the effect of falling water we employed a method described by Malcolm Furlow in *Model Railroader* magazine. He recommends using angel hair, which is a material used in the filters for fish tanks. He suggested using the straight variety rather than the curly type but our local pet shop only had the latter. We found that by wetting it, it straightened out quite well and lengths of this were laid down the length of the falls from top to bottom. As we got lower we spread the hair out just as the water does in waterfalls. The angel hair was stuck in place with white glue. Not very much of the hair is required as a little seems to go a long way.

The bed of the river was sprinkled with a mix of HO and N scale stone ballast with a little sand thrown in. This was spread around leaving the colour of the chipboard to show through in places as well. Again everything was well stuck down with glue. To pour the river the baseboard was carried out into the garden one very hot summer afternoon. Apart from enjoying the good weather there were two reasons for this. The casting resin we use has a very strong smell and is not recommended for indoor use unless the room is very well ventilated. Secondly the hot sunshine would help to dry out the resin more quickly. The first layer was tinted with a blue-green colour to try to capture the colour of mountain water. The next two layers were clear. Normally the resin takes a while to dry out but with the hot sun and with extra hardener it set fairly quickly. The layout section was then turned onto its back so that the waterfall could be poured. However when we

poured the resin, tinted a very faint blue, we found that it would not cover the angel hair. We overcame this difficulty by getting two large tubes of Uhu adhesive, putting the layout right way up again and running the Uhu down the falls. Surprisingly it worked despite our doubts. The last stage was to pour the upper level of the river, the bed having been prepared in the same way as the lower section. As we poured the resin we allowed it to flow over the waterfall and down to spread over the lower section. The result is surprisingly good. In fact at one recent exhibition a lady apologised because her small son had broken a tree on the layout when he put his finger into the river to see if the water was real!

Talking of trees, those in the gorge have trunks made from balsa wood dowelling shaped to a long taper, painted brown-red and then drilled at various points around and along the length of the trunk. Pieces of Asparagus Fern are stuck to those holes and the result are quite creditable pine trees. The only problem is that the fern eventually fades but we have re-sprayed the foliage with matt medium and covered with Woodlands grass or weed scenic dressing mix. This not only brings them back to life but also thickens up the foliage realistically.

The bridge is a Pola curved steel type and at the tunnel end the supports are built into the side of the gorge so that the trains run directly onto the bridge from the tunnel. Strictly speaking because the bridge is steel and curved it should have a central supporting pier, a fact that has been pointed out to us by some civil engineers. However, on balance we decided that a large support would spoil the gorge and so we have dispensed with it. At the moment the bridge is undergoing maintenance as can be seen by the scaffolding at one end and the painter working his way along the handrails.

Above the gorge are the farm houses or chalets. These are standard Kibri kits with some superdetailing. The hay has been gathered into small stacks in the field; these have been modelled with cocktail sticks with cotton wool wrapped around, dipped into a one to one white glue and water mix and then put into a dish containing Noch electrostatic grass. We have used a yellow-green to simulate drying hay. A few Preiser figures dotted around complete the picture.

In our article on modelling small scenes (also in this book) we have described various other areas of the layout together with details of the construction of these scenes.

Modelling small scenes

David and Mike Polglaze

In our description of the construction of the scenery in Rheinfalle Gorge on our H0 scale metre gauge Swiss layout 'Die Bernhardinbahn' we mentioned the idea of theme scenes or centres of interest within the scenery. This is a concept which has been developed by Dave Frary and other American modellers. The idea is that the layout should be modelled as a series of scenes, each of which forms a centre of interest for the viewer. The scenes will vary in theme and their size and shape; they can be relatively complete in themselves, rather like the dioramas so popular

with military modellers. They should provide variety but should complement and not clash with adjacent scenes. The less detailed transitional zones between these centres of interest, sometimes supplemented by visual barriers such as trees and buildings, tend to separate the scenes. Thus the viewer's attention will be held in one area while he studies all the details. He then passes on to other scenes and repeats the process.

There are several advantages to this scheme. An important one is that it will make the layout appear larger than it is. Also by concentrating the

Below left *In this view of part of 'Die Bernhardinbahn' layout there are several small separate scenes forming centres of interest scenically. The scenes are linked by the road and the railway which help to carry the viewer's eye from one scene to another.*
Below right *The large tree between path and railway. Note the exposed roots where the bank has crumbled away.*

Left *We can employ some of the principles of photographic and art composition in our scenic modelling to guide the viewer to the scene we wish him or her to look at. Here the two trees framing the scene at either side and the footpath curving up into the centre lead the viewer's eye inevitably to the group of passengers waiting for the train behind the crossing sign.*

Above left *The cement silos at Hinterrhein Station were built from a Kibri kit. The base is real concrete.*
Above right *Frau Grosse sits on her doorstep watching the passing traffic while her husband works in the garden.*
Below *A lorry driver has to wait, patiently or otherwise, while the herd of cows passes him on the road. In true Swiss fashion the cows are fitted with bells around their necks.*

Top left *The pedestrian crossing with passengers leaving the station and the cars stopped to allow them to cross form another little detail scene within the overall scenery.*

Above left *The roadworks where the road is being widened. Note the lighter area of rock where the rock face has been blasted and cut away. The bulldozer is a modified Wiking model.*

Top right *Hinterrhein station building is a wooden kit structure. Note the many small details including the letter box, timetable, 'glokens' and window boxes complete with plants, which add interest and realism to the model.*

Above right *Below the roadworks the road winds downhill. Note the marker posts showing the edge of the road.*

detailing in specific areas, where it will be observed and appreciated to the full, rather than spreading it more thinly over the whole layout you will achieve the maximum effect from the work you put in. This is not to say that the standard of the scenic work should be less good in the areas between the centres of interest, merely that there will be less detail. Taken overall the result should be a well composed landscape model made up of separate but linked scenes.

We have adopted this principle on our layout and readers may be interested to take a closer look at some of the theme scenes we have modelled within the overall scenic setting of the railway.

Before describing the construction of these in detail we should perhaps make a few general comments about the techniques and materials we employ. We have based our methods of scenery modelling on the system devised by Dave Frary in which all the paints and adhesives used are water soluble; this makes scenery building quick, easy, clean and very effective. We haven't followed his method word for word but have experimented and come up with our own variations which suit European modelling and the materials available in Britain.

The materials we use are readily obtainable. Almost all the grass we use is from the Woodlands

The hairpin bend in the road with the railway above and behind just running onto the arch bridge. The first two piers for the bridge which will carry the new road across the valley are on the right.

A closer view showing the details. Note the wooden shuttering for the pier on the right ready for the concrete to be poured, with a completed pier behind it to the left. The 'road works' sign was scratchbuilt following an example sketched in Switzerland.

The sawmill in the old quarry. The plastic logs in the kit have been replaced by twigs cut into suitable sizes.

Among the many small details included in the sawmill scene is the open door on this lorry with the driver about to climb into the cab.

The sawmill is a Kibri kit which is complete with interior detailing including machinery. Roof is removable to enable the interior to be displayed.

Scenics range. For basic earth colour we employ the earth mix described in the article on building Rheinfalle Gorge (also in this book). For earth in gardens, footpaths, and so on we use the real thing. Tins are filled from the garden and the earth is dried out and then run through a fine mesh tea strainer. We have two of these strainers, one with a very fine mesh and another rather coarser. This provides us with two grades of soil. As far as possible all timber is made from twigs giving a much better result than plastic. To fix all these things down we use 'wet water' as described in the Rheinfalle Gorge article together with matt medium. This latter is correctly known in Britain as 'acrylic medium' and the type we use is Nacryl new art acrylic medium (matt) made by Winsor & Newton. It isn't cheap, but we water it down to about a 6:1 mix (water:medium) and apply it with a spray bottle. As bought, the medium is very thick but we mix it in an old jug and store it in 1.5 litre wine bottles. One bottle holds about half the watered down medium. The advantage of this material over white glue is that the matt medium dries without leaving any trace whatsoever.

Whenever possible we try to work from photographs, not with the idea of making an exact copy but because the pictures are so useful in getting the details and colouring right. Because we cannot pop over to Switzerland whenever we want to check a detail or three (if only we could!), we make the most of our short visits on holiday. Not only do we take numerous photographs, we also always carry a notebook in which small details can be jotted down or sketched, not just about the railway but also regarding general scenic items. It is amazing how much you see that if it is not noted down at the time is soon forgotten. A rough sketch often helps; it needn't be artistic so long as it shows the information you want. Even if we are just out for a day with the family the notebook is

always with us. We have made notes on such things as pathway markings, road signs, including the painted ones, the fact that most seats on footpaths have a litter bin near them, and so many other little details that are normally taken for granted. They all help to bring realism to a model and, incidentally, very often present quite a challenge in trying to find something to make them from.

Let us now have a closer look at some of the photographs of the theme scenes working our way along the layout. The first shows a tree standing between the station and the edge of the baseboard. The tree is on top of a small earth bank which is showing signs of falling down, allowing some of the tree roots to be exposed. The pathway from the Rheinfalle leads up past the tree to Hinterrhein Station. The 'X' warning sign can be seen just in front of the tracks. The 'X' was cut from a continental road sign sheet and attached to a piece of N gauge rail painted red and white. The bank was built up first, using plaster, and the tree was bedded into the plaster while it was still wet. The tree was made up from three suitable twigs which were wired together to give the maximum amount of branch spread. The trunk was built up using Milliput which, when dry was scored to represent bark and painted a grey-brown colour. The foliage which was put on at a later stage is lichen but this is due to be replaced by Woodlands foliage. After the bank had dried out the area was covered with earth mix, itself covered while still wet with real earth. To apply this or grass onto a steep slope is not always easy so we use a postcard folded lengthways into a 'V' with the earth or grass spooned in and then gently blown over the required area. Bits of twig were used to model the exposed roots, being glued into suitable places on the bank. The footpath was made from real earth spread over earth mix and stuck down with matt medium. When well and truly dried out the pathway was rubbed with a finger (or a track rubber) to give the appearance of hard packed earth. The area around is covered with grass and this was spread around dry, using various shades, until it looked right and then sprayed with matt medium to fix it in place. Whenever using the mix we spray the whole area first with 'wet water'. This soaks the surface and helps to carry the matt medium down into the grass.

The cement silos are a Kibri kit which was made up and then sprayed silver all over using Woolworth cans of car spray undercoat. Before the structure was installed a concrete base was needed. There are several ways to do this, the most usual being to put down a flat surface and cover it with concrete paint (Humbrol). However we wanted something more realistic so we made a proper concrete raft. Cement and sand were put through the coarse tea strainer and mixed with N gauge ballast in the correct proportions (1:3:6 — teaspoons). Shuttering made from strips of balsa wood was put in and the concrete was poured, levelled and allowed to set. While the concrete was still wet the offloading valves, taken from an old Hornby cement wagon, were set into it. The silos were later glued into position with a couple of suitable Preiser figures in orange overalls and hard hats placed on them. Underneath is a Kibri DAF bulk cement lorry. This was assembled as in the kit instructions but the air lines between the tractor unit and trailer were added and the fifth wheel coupling was covered in grease. The grass was brought up to two sides and a road was put in on the third side.

In the next scene a herd of cows is being driven to higher pastures. They are passing a lorry on its way down to the valley which has had to stop for the animals. The driver is leaning out of his cab, no doubt hurling abuse at the farmer. The cab

window has been carefully removed and a suitable Preiser figure has been fitted into the cab after painting. Being warm weather he is stripped to the waist. Most of the cows have bells around their necks; if only we could reproduce the sound as well. The bells were made from the heads of square copper nails fixed to the necks with super glue. The leather halters around the necks are just black lines put on with a Rotring drawing pen. Behind the cows on the road some of their 'trade marks' can be seen. Also here is a chalet just above the road with its garden, still not completed, and Frau Grosse sitting on the doorstep. Like most of the figures on the layout she is one of the Preiser family. We bought a box of 120 unpainted figures and as one is wanted a suitable candidate is selected, painted and put in position. We don't confine ourselves to Preiser, however, but use all sorts including the 00 scale figures, which are slightly bigger than the H0 ones, but then we humans come in a variety of sizes anyway.

Moving down the road we come to Hinterrhein Station. The building is a wooden kit made by the Swiss firm, Fides, but available over here. The structure when made up needs colouring and we found the best way to get the brown colour we wanted was to use creosote. Various details were added including the letter box found on almost every Swiss station. The 'glokens' are brass castings made by Bemo. Under the windows at the end of the building are the stacks of wood ready for use in the winter. These are made up of very small pieces of pine cut to about the right size and glued into place. Each log was fitted into position with a pair of tweezers and a spot of white glue diluted one to one with water. The window boxes are Lego bricks and the plants were modelled from Woodlands long grass soaked in white glue and put in place with tweezers. Once dry the flowers are added by stippling white on the grass

The farmhouse above the quarry at the edge of a pine forest. The many added details include human and animal figures from the Preiser range. At the right of the picture a group are cutting up wood for the winter fires.

A closer view of the woodcutting group. The figures are by Preiser and the wood is real wood cut from small twigs.

or foliage. When this has dried we go over the white with bright reds and other colours.

On the other side of the level crossing we come to the site of road works, where the road is being widened and straightened to remove a series of hairpin bends. This particular scene was built after the scenic work on this part of the layout had been carried out and to make it the original rock face was 'blasted out' with a Stanley knife and small chisel. A new rock face was then cast in. The pile of rubble being removed was made up from odd bits and pieces of plaster broken up and glued in position. Because the surface has been cut recently and has not been exposed to the elements it is a much lighter colour than the original rock. Again the figures are Preiser. The bulldozer is a Wiking model which has been cut in half just in front of the cab and rebuilt as one of the types which pivots in the middle. It has been dirtied up with mud on the wheels and a fair amount of dirt and grime everywhere else. The flashing warning lights are by Brawa.

Just around the corner can be seen the first two piers that will eventually carry the new road on a bridge across the valley. One pier is complete but the other is still waiting for the concrete to be poured. The shuttering is in position but it will be noticed that it has no scaffolding around it, the reason being that this is another job waiting to be done when we have time! To the left can be seen one of the large road works signs used in Switzerland. Above the road the railway line can be seen with a Schneider home/distant signal by the tunnel mouth.

The old quarry is now used by a sawmill which is not connected to the railway. The sawmill is a Kibri kit, not an easy one to build but realistic and

well detailed when completed. The plastic tree trunks and logs have all been discarded and replaced by real wood which looks so much better. The quarry face was made from rock mouldings in the same way as the gorge walls were modelled. The railway is carried across the valley on a stone arch viaduct. This was made from wood cut to shape and covered with Faller embossed stone paper. It is at this point that the line runs above the sawmill on a ledge and then into the St Bernhardin Tunnel and thus back to the hidden sidings.

Above the quarry is a large farmhouse and the edge of a pine forest. The people at the farm, yes Preiser again, are getting ready for winter by cutting up logs for stacking. The logs and cut firewood are pine twigs cut up and then split with a modelling knife. The sawdust and little bits were saved from the sawing up of other pieces of timber and put through the coarse tea strainer. Everything was glued down with matt medium, including the earth around the building. The road which passes the farm is modelled with N gauge ballast well stuck down with a little grass down the middle of it.

Putting detail onto models not only helps to bring the layout to life but can give the builder hours of fun in the process. Try to do something a little different from usual, but based on observation of the real thing. We have a lorry parked by the sawmill, but ours has one cab door open and the driver just climbing in; the post bus by the station has one of its indicators working; and so on. Although this is a continental layout the same principles and rules apply to any model be it British, German or Outer Mongolian, so don't forget to keep that notebook handy!

Eitomo — an East African narrow gauge (009) model railway

Howard Coulson

I had two reasons for building an East African model. I had spent 18 months in Kenya and wanted a three dimensional souvenir and I wanted a spectacular setting for 'mainline narrow gauge' in 009, instead of the common branchlines, quarries or rabbit warrens. Eitomo serves as a working diorama to display rarely or never previously modelled narrow gauge locomotives and stock.

Eitomo is located in the East African Highlands, on the border between Kenya and Tanganyika, near Lake Victoria. The line is sited on the route of a proposed feeder line from Mohuru Bay, on Lake Victoria, to Mau Summit on the Uganda Railway line from Nakuru to Kisumu. The gauge is a nominal 2ft 6in. Several such railways were built in many parts of Africa (in contrast to the less common but better known South African 2ft lines) to act as feeders to the metre, 3ft 6in or standard gauge main lines.

The site is envisaged as a crossing station and locomotive watering point, built purely for railway operating purposes, miles from any habitation. Eitomo is in the Nandi Mountains about 60 miles from Mau. The name Eitomo does not appear on any map of the area because this 'African' name is made up of the first two letters respectively of the christian names of my wife,

son and daughter! The layout was planned as the maximum size single board which I could get in my car; this worked out as 5ft 6in × 2ft 6in. I was able to use 12in radius curves compared with the 9in or even 6in radius curves so often seen on 009 layouts at that time (1977). The scenic setting is a conglomerate based on photographs and memories of different parts of the East African Highlands.

Planning

The creation of this East African scene involved reconsideration of factors which are taken for granted when modelling the British scene.

1 Scenic features Should be spectacularly rocky and dry. A natural rock 'tunnel' from Tanganyika was perfect for hiding the track curve at one end of the layout — plenty of access is available for track cleaning.

2 Colour Having decided on modelling the dry season, the foliage should be dry, with just a little green near the drippings from the water crane. In much of Kenya the earth is a bright red colour and this must be shown. The earth colour on the model is toned down a little because those who have not been to Kenya would never believe the colour! As a result the dominant colour is red,

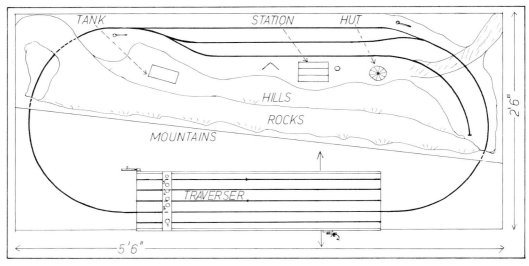

Fig 2 Creating the backdrop.

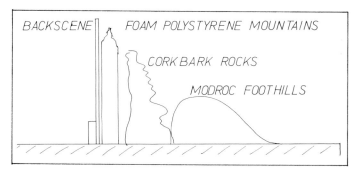

which gives a good contrast with the green of English layouts at exhibitions.

3 Population As many African natives and creatures as possible are represented. Although the station is in the middle of nowhere, as in the prototype a good number of Africans are gathered at the station. Set pieces depicting various happenings are incorporated to keep up interest between trains and to add atmosphere.

4 Structures These are few! One native hut, but no village, and a small corrugated iron station building.

5 Railway No high technology or main line gadgetry here; ungated crossings and no signals are the correct order of things.

6 Lighting A single spotlight is used to enhance the dry nature of the scene and give the impression of the hot sun beating down. If nothing else it manages to make the operators feel thirsty!

Scenics

The baseboard is of conventional construction, that is 2in × 1in timber framing surfaced with ½in chipboard. The scenery then goes on top.

Left *Fig 1* Plan view of 'Eitomo' layout.

Right *An impressive Garratt articulated locomotive waits to haul a passenger train on from Eitomo. The engine has a scratchbuilt body mounted on two 0-6-0 N gauge chassis and is one of a number of interesting and authentic models of African prototypes on the layout.*

The plan of the layout (Fig 1) shows the rock face going across the layout almost diagonally. This ensures that the view of the layout changes greatly as you move along it. The rocky background is built up like a stage set. It consists of a flat foreground backed by three low relief scenic zones. When seen from the front this gives an illusion of considerable depth, and enhances the view of the train in its setting (Fig 2).

After the track had been laid, wired up and tested, scenic work was started. Mod-roc foothills were built up on rolled up newspaper, according to the makers instructions. The rear was shaped vertically to bed into the rockface. The rockface is built up of cork bark which was bought from a florist so that very large pieces could be used. The cork bark was carefully split and laid in place to give the effect of rock strata. The cork was secured in position with screws and glue. Suitable pieces of the bark were very carefully chosen to build up the rock tunnel feature.

The mountain section was carved from polystyrene foam insulation board. The visible part was hacked to shape with a bread knife to leave a

Left *The large station nameboard, complete with elevation above sea level, is typical of East African railways. The livestock wagons are conversions of Airfix cattle wagon kits to narrow gauge. The hunter in the upper left of the picture is beside a termite hill, a common feature of the East African landscape.*

Right *Rock faces were modelled with carefully chosen pieces of cork bark covered with the scenic 'goo' made up as described in the text. The zebra at lower left is one of many animals included on the layout.*

coarse surface with mountain peaks. The foam polystyrene was fixed to the cork bark with screws and tile cement.

The next stage was to coat everything except for the rails and sleepers with scenic 'goo'. This is made from Polyfilla, powder paints (red, brown and black), Resin W and water mixed to a paintable consistency. Small batches of the 'goo' were used so that the colour varies slightly over the layout. The tops of the foothills and rock face were painted with the mixture and, where appropriate, flock powders were sprinkled on while the 'goo' was still wet. Great care was taken on the rock tunnel to get the colour shades to make the cork bark look like rock and not bark. Lighter shades of the mixture were applied to the mountain backscene and light grey shadowing was added. This colouring toning makes the backscene appear to recede and contributes to the illusion of depth. Similarly, the flock powders were

selected so that the brighter greens were used in the shadier and damper areas while faded colours were employed for the drier parts. The colour differences are essential in enhancing the relief and in giving the hot, dry, African look. Extra ballast covered in 'goo' was placed by the tracks to represent local shingle or stones. The road is also of earth, of slightly darker colour. It was shaped with a wet brush to get the edges correct and the surface fairly level. Before the road dried ruts were scraped in to represent the usual churned up mud surface.

Termite hills are common features of the East African landscape. These were modelled by driving panel pins in to the surface of the baseboard or hills and coating them with the scenic 'goo'. The termite hills on the layout are under scale size since scale versions of twenty feet high mounds in this model setting would destroy the carefully calculated scenic depth effect.

Structures and vegetation

Although there are few structures on this layout those present have been carefully chosen. There are no signals, no signal box and no platforms. The station building is in 'African corrugated iron', and is modelled on that at Makwiro in Rhodesia. It was built from plastic corrugated sheeting and plastic card. It does not sit on brick foundations but on a raised wooden floor supported by pilings. The building is painted light cream to help keep it cool, and it sits quite naturally between two 'hill' spurs.

The native hut is really there to show that the setting is Africa and not a safari park, zoo or the Wild West as are sometimes suggested! The hut was built from dried flower stalks stuck to a toilet roll core with plenty of the scenic 'goo'. It took much longer to make than the station building but I am very pleased with the effect.

The third major structure is the water tank, which justifies the very existence of Eitomo. It is a smaller version of the East African Railways water tanks at Voi. The tank sides are from Mikes Models and the supporting girders are from Faller. A corrugated iron cover has been added to reduce evaporation. The smaller structures include two Mikes Models TT3 NER water cranes, American type railroad crossing signs, Station Road and bus stop signs and a British pillar box. The most important item is typically African, the very large station name board which carries both the station name and the altitude above sea level.

Having chosen a dry location in the dry season, modelling the trees and shrubs was relatively easy. Various coloured lichens, mainly reds and yellows, have been used to represent the dry shrub or undergrowth. Green lichens have been employed in shady or moist areas. Trees have been modelled in several ways; dried twigs coated

Left *The foothills are seen in the foreground with the mountains behind. The use of lighter shades of the basic colours together with light grey shadowing has created a realistic impression of distance for the mountains.*

Right *This natural rock bridge or tunnel, based on one in Tanganyika, is a very attractive scenic feature and is effective in disguising the curve at the end of the layout leading back to the fiddle yard behind the hills.*

The native hut, scratchbuilt as described in the text, with the ex-US Army station bus.

The scene of the derailment complete with escaping animals. The water crane is a Mikes Models TT3 NER cast metal kit model.

Vegetation is mainly lichen of various shades together with dried flower heads and trees made from twigs coated with flock powders. Some commercial tree models were also used.

Eitomo station building is modelled on Makwiro in Rhodesia and was built from plastic corrugated sheet and plastic sheet. The structure does not have brick foundations but is supported by wooden pilings.

in flock powders to give the rather grotesque natural shapes and colours, some purchased tree models which did not look European but suit Eitomo, and dried flower heads which look like some of the more exotic African flora. There are areas of concentrated plantings which contrast well with the bare rocks. Any plantings on the rock faces are smaller than elsewhere to give the effect of distance.

Population

There are a large number of figures in the scene, since the station would act as a gathering point — I have never seen a deserted station. Many proprietary figures have been used and modified to give a number of Africans and Europeans. I still need to add some Asians, particularly Sikhs with their conspicuous turbans. The figures are arranged in groups to be more realistic: **1** A group of Africans, sitting and standing by the station bus (an ex-US Army truck) — one woman has a basket balanced on her head. **2** 'David Shepherd' painting a portrait of an elephant, with an audience. **3** 'David Attenborough' film team filming gorillas. This group is on top of the rock tunnel, with a large gorilla which many say is King Kong. **4** Station Master 'treed' up the water tower with a lion at the bottom (plus a hunter stalking the lion, plus another lion stalking the hunter). **5** A spectacular derailment in the siding, with a rhino rescuing its mate and also releasing a crocodile — many children ask me if I know there has been a derailment. **6** There are one or two genuine passengers waiting — the shorts-clad party of hikers were perfect for these. There is also a postman with a Royal Mail van, which surprises many people but is correct for the period modelled.

I have been lucky enough to find some Airfix zoo animals figure sets which, with careful painting, can be used to represent many African animals. But note that, this being Africa, there are no tigers, no bears, no alligators, no

kangaroos and no dinosaurs! Many people do recognise the animals, and there is often debate on whether the elephants are African or Indian. Perhaps there are too many animals and incidents packed in to such a small area but they do give some of the atmosphere of East Africa and entertain the public. To complete the scene I do need some 4mm scale vultures, but these are not available!

Vehicles, locomotives and stock

Road vehicles are fairly easy to provide as at the period modelled the most common vehicles were Morris Minors, Landrovers and Jeeps. Proprie-

Above right *The water tower is based on the East African Railways water tanks at Voi. The model tank has sides made with Mikes Models parts and supporting girders by Faller; the corrugated iron cover helps to reduce evaporation.*

Right *The locomotive fuel tank utilises a tank from a military vehicle kit together with a supporting frame, ladder and extra details made up from bits and pieces from the scrap box.*

There are many small detailed scenes within the overall scenery to add interest for viewers at exhibitions. One of these is the 'David Attenborough' film team stalking the large gorilla known to the locals as 'King Kong'.

Another is 'David Shepherd' painting one of his famous elephant pictures.

tary models or kits can be found for all of these. The station bus (ex-US Army) is a kit and it too is appropriate. I have been in such a 'bus' in Tanganyika.

Locomotives and stock were frequently transferred from one line to another, sometimes after regauging. A successful design was often used on more than one railway. Designs from many countries; Great Britain, Belgium, France, Germany, Italy, Switzerland, Japan, Canada, the United States, and others have been used in Africa, including military types. There is no justification for freelance modelling in an African setting when there is such a range of actual prototypes from which to choose; somewhere in darkest Africa there will be the locomotive or vehicle you want to model! The range goes from 0-4-0 to 4-8-4 + 4-8-4 and from 4wD to BoBo + BoBo, and if, like me, you are interested in articulated locomotives you will find prototypes for most designs working in the dark continent. My locomotives represent just a tiny fraction of what there is to model.

Rolling stock is typically African with passenger vehicles in cream livery, some fitted with sunshades over the windows. A little real life politics creeps in too, with 'Natives only' or 'Coloured only' passenger stock — some lines just added fourth class. Railcars are well represented, both on the model and the prototype. On some long lines the journey time was cut by fifty percent by the use of express railcars; many passenger trains were mixed passenger and freight and were very slow. On the narrower gauges, express (non-stop) trains were virtually non-existent because of the absence of signals on single line systems. The most common method of working was by telephone/telegraph with written train orders. Freight vehicles cover a wide range of types and are usually bogie wagons rather than small four wheel wagons as on the British narrow gauge. Every train should stop at the loop at Eitomo, from seconds to hours until permission to proceed has been granted. Since the line is worked by train order and ticket there are no token exchange facilities as on British single track lines.

Two of the typically East African railcars operated on the layout.

Operation

As built, the fiddle yard was three track with two railcar spurs (Fig 3). Only one full length train could be held and variety was very limited, so after a few months, the fiddle yard was replaced by a five track traverser. Two of the tracks were split electrically so that seven trains could be held. The traverser had a simple handle pull which made it very easy to jerk the traverser and derail every item of stock. This traverser was replaced by a much improved version. The new traverser slides in ½in plastic U-sections with the sliders being ½in square hardwood mouldings. Traverser movement is by a screw — a length of threaded rod. The screw pitch is very fine so that there is no jerking of the stock but a great deal of turning is required. Some people think that I am cranking a generator to drive the trains! The traverser has high sides to avoid trains being caught by the operator's sleeves. The sides support a cross-member which carries push-to-make switches for each track except for the 'main line'. The main line is powered via a bolt on the baseboard to a socket on the traverser to give a continuous run facility.

There is a capacity of seven trains on the traverser plus two or three railcars which are placed on the track at the rear and driven round

Fig 3 Plan of the original fiddle yard.

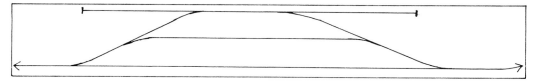

Above *The traverser described in detail in the text. The backscene divider has been removed for this picture.*
Left *The traverser in use at an exhibition fully loaded with locomotives and rolling stock. Note the handle used to move the traverser to select the track required.*

whilst the traverser is moved to the next position. This operation results in a simple sequence of about twelve train movements, lasting ten to fifteen minutes, which is quite adequate for exhibitions. If the operator is occupied talking to the public then he can use the continuous run option.

What about the public reaction to a layout which to me represents East Africa? I have met two people who insisted that they have travelled on the line — with a Mozambique locomotive and South West African coaches. And at each exhibition I usually meet people who have lived in or visited East Africa. Their usual reaction is that the layout brings back memories but that they can't quite place the location. It is very pleasing when a narrow gauge enthusiast recognises the stock and locomotives I have built. As with all railway modelling success depends upon creating the right atmosphere and that is the real challenge in modelling overseas railways.

A model dock

David Andress

When planning our 6ft by 4ft 00 scale layout I was very keen to include a harbour and dock. The links between the railways and shipping have always been very important for the real railways and there are also many benefits for the modeller. I have seen harbours and docks on a number of model railway layouts at exhibitions and in the model press and have been very impressed with them as scenic features. The models have varied from large facilities with ocean-going ships to small broken down wharves with a barge or two so there is plenty of scope for choice. It is certainly not necessary to have a lot of space available; a simple but interesting dock can be fitted in on even the smallest of layouts. Scenically any modelled water is usually attractive and when we add ships or boats, wharves or jetties, cranes and warehouses, and the many other details typical of these areas the potential is very great indeed. Of course you will always want to provide one or more sidings to serve the dock and this will add to the operational possibilities on your layout with extra shunting and additional traffic.

On our Westport Branch layout the harbour was designed to be the central feature with the continuous oval type track plan around it. This not only makes good use of the central part of the layout, which is relatively inaccessible for other purposes, but also provides a scenic break between the two sides of the layout. This visually separates the station area from the rest of the line and makes the layout appear larger. The central harbour, together with a hill in one corner of the layout through which the railway tunnels, also helps to disguise the round and round nature of the continuous oval track plan and give the illusion that the line really does go somewhere. The separation of the two sides of the layout is further achieved by a river leading into the harbour at one side and the outlet to the sea, spanned by a lifting bridge for the railway line, at the other.

The features of a dock area will vary depending on the size and complexity of the facility and with the type of trade carried on; fishing, coal, sand, gravel, general cargo, oil, containers, and so on. We chose to model a small port handling coastal trade with a dock for general cargo and a jetty serving a small oil storage depot with facilities for

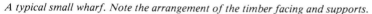

A typical small wharf. Note the arrangement of the timber facing and supports.

transfer to railway oil tank wagons. If you are planning a dock for your layout it is worthwhile looking at some of the small docks and wharves to be seen around the coast. You will get many ideas and basing your model on the real thing, even if you make many modifications to suit your needs, will result in a more authentic and realistic scene. One of the accompanying photographs shows a small wharf of typical construction and I used this as a guide when building Westport. On layouts one often sees models of warehouses of the older style, typified by the example modelled by John Ahern and included in the range of structure plans he drew up. Though very attractive I wanted something a bit different and rather more modern for Westport and I found an appropriate type of corrugated iron building on the wharf at Poole, shown in one of the photographs. However this structure was too large for the space I had available so would have to be reduced in size.

The following description of the construction of the harbour and dock for Westport may be of interest. Obviously you would need to make changes to suit your own requirements if you want to build a harbour for your own layout. Because the harbour was the central theme of the layout, both in concept and in geographical location the layout was planned around it. Baseboard construction was designed to accommodate a depressed area on which the water in the river, harbour and outlet to the sea could be modelled. Thus the framework utilised a 4in by 1in outer frame with cross pieces of 2in by 1in timber arranged to give a top 'ground' level at 4in and a lower 'water' level at 2in above the lower edge of the baseboard. Soft wood fibre insulation board was then fixed onto the framework with the harbour, river and outlet area cut out from the ground level and mounted at the lower level. The basic shapes of the banks of the river and shores of the harbour were then modelled using Mod-Roc plaster bandage material to fill in the spaces

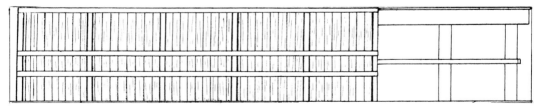

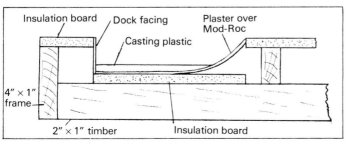

Rock faces

Richard Wyatt

If one is modelling an area known for its rocky or mountainous countryside, we expect to have to reproduce rock faces on some part of the model, but with the tendency of railway lines to cut into the landscape, bare rock is often exposed in parts of the country not renowned for its rockiness. Therefore, it is likely that most modellers will be faced with the task of representing exposed rock at some time.

As with many things on the scenic side of a model railway, a rock face will convince most viewers if it looks realistic and is in keeping with the rest of the model; this latter is very important as it is essential for any model rock face to look as though it would be there on the full size landscape. The question we must always ask ourselves when planning to construct a rock face on any part of our model is, 'If I was looking at a real landscape, would I expect to see a rock face in that place? and how would it appear?'

The modeller who is keen for his rock faces to reflect accurately those found in the area on which his model is based, will need some understanding of the local geology and a good collection of photographs of exposed rock in the area. Even within a relatively small area there are often considerable variations in the appearance of rock faces, since the type of rock varies with depth below the surface and weathering varies with the length of time exposed. Rock strata are often tilted so that different types of rock break the surface close together, with the softer rock wearing away to leave outcrops of the harder rock. Rock outcrops will probably have been exposed to the weather for many thousands of years causing changes in colour and rounding off of sharp corners, even in the hardest of rocks, whereas railway cuttings, quarries etc, have exposed the rock much more recently and consequently the weather has had much less effect.

Although there are many types of rock with wide ranges of colouring, texture and appearance, these fall into five general types for the purpose of modelling.

1 The softer rocks, not normally exposed except on the coast, and which, though substantial enough not to collapse, are comparatively crumbly when exposed in railway cuttings (eg, chalk in South-East England). There is sometimes a high soil content which allows the growth of grass and foliage, usually encouraged by a railway company, as it improves stability.

2 The outcrops of hard rock found in such places as Dartmoor, North Wales, West Scotland and the Lake District. These may be areas at the tops of mountains, or outcrops somewhere on the lower slopes surrounded by grass. It is these latter towards which the attention of the modeller will be directed as their size can be anything from a few square yards upwards, unlike the former which are far too large to model.

3 The man made rock faces cut into hard rock for quarries and railway cuttings. Blasted rock will be more shattered and have more crevices than hewn rock, but faces will be almost sheer, with the rough edges virtually unaffected by weathering. This is the type of rock face most commonly seen on a model.

4 Loose scree such as is found on the slopes of many mountains in Wales and elsewhere, and

Fig 1 Stratified rock breaking the surface.

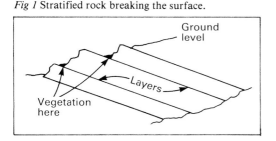

Fig 2 Stratified rock in a cliff face.

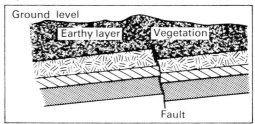

Left *Llanymawddwy locomotive shed and yard showing the gravel in cellulose filler method of modelling rock faces. The raised ground with road between the locomotive yard and the section of the main line behind helps to separate the two tracks visually giving a greater effect of distance in the model. Note the diesel oil tank, made from a military vehicle kit, and the scrapped quarry wagons behind it.*

in straight lines with rocks in the middle. North Wales and the Yorkshire Dales are two obvious locations but there are many others.

Just as the appearance of exposed rock surfaces varies, so will modelling techniques vary also. Two or more different modelling techniques can often be utilised on the same layout to good effect, and a combination of two methods will sometimes produce a rock formation suitable for a particular situation. In a model, a rock cutting can be made much steeper than an earth one and consequently can be used as a means of saving space, though not as much as may appear at first, due to the thickness of scenery constructed as rock faces.

Before dealing with the actual reproduction of rock faces in model form, I would emphasise again the need to actually go and look at similar features and note carefully such things as evidence of strata, changes in rock type with depth, the actual appearance of the rock, any vegetation, whether there is loose rock at the foot, whether the face is usually wet or dry, and so on. When dealing with quarries, consideration needs to be given to access to any intermediate levels and

also along several parts of our coastline. Soft or brittle rocks (eg, shale or slate) breaking away in large quantities from the main formation is the cause, but for modelling purposes, tips of slate and mine waste etc, fall into this category.

5 River banks, which often include groups of large and small boulders, and some sizeable lumps of rock around which the river has to wind. Depending on how far up the hillside, the route of the stream can vary from tortuous to more or less

A lovely view of Ivor *with a passenger train approaching Llanymawddwy station on the way down the valley. Some gravel in filler rock faces can be seen and at the right rear of the picture the edge of the quarry modelled with real stone. The lake is only 15mm below the rail level. The reflections in the water give a very realistic effect.*

Right *The quarry was modelled with pieces of real stone pressed into cellulose filler, giving a realistically rugged appearance. The crane is from the Mikes Models range of cast metal kits. Earl hauls a train of loaded wagons away from the quarry. (Photograph by R. Wyatt).*

Below right *A view down the incline into the disused quarry at the lower end of the layout. The incline is modelled with carved Polyfilla, the building was made up from Das and the rock faces in the quarry and on the river bank are from pieces of real stone.*

the nature of the quarry floor. Streams in particular, need a lot of attention and many photographs if a realistic representation is to be made. It is very difficult to model realistically from memory without information to hand.

Turning now to methods of producing the desired rock face on a model, I personally have used four of the methods described below, but there are a couple of others which can be used to good effect, so I include them to make the overall picture more complete. The main modelling materials and processes are: cork bark; real stone; fine gravel in cellulose filler; sculptured modelling compound; sculptured plaster; and sculptured polystyrene.

Cork Bark

Pieces of cork bark can be purchased from model shops and also some florists shops. The gnarled and creviced appearance is most suited to the well weathered outcrops of rock mentioned in **2** above. In fact, in my opinion, it is the best material to realistically catch the appearance of this type of rock.

As purchased, the cork bark is brown in colour, curved (since tree trunks are round) and fairly thick (15mm to 30mm). Because of the two last, I always take the effort to carve out as much as possible of the substance of the bark behind the surface layer; this makes the remainder, which contains all the necessary detail, much more flexible, enabling it to be straightened out, or curved even more, as required. If the rockwork is being applied to an existing scenery base, as usually happens in my case, the reduction in

Right *Single Fairlie* Gowrie *curves across the viaduct to the entrance to Llanymawddwy station. The river bed was modelled as decribed in the text. Careful planning of the contours of the scenery has created a very realistic landscape.*

Aber Rhiwlech station is enclosed by hills justifying the cramped arrangement of station and sidings. Rock faces were modelled using the gravel in cellulose filler technique. The many small details bring the scene to life.

Below left *Fig 3* Rock outcrop on a hillside.

Below right *Fig 4* Modelling rock outcrops (in section).

Above right *Fig 5* Use of real stone for cliffs, quarries and railway cuttings.

thickness enables the cork to be far less prominent when fixed to the scenic base. If I build the scenery base around the rockwork (which cannot be altered) there is a danger of spilling other materials onto the finished surface. Despite the additional flexibility, the bark will still be a bit too springy to stick easily to any surface and should be helped with a couple of pins until the glue has set. I normally stick the bark in place with PVA glue and once the bark is secure, build up around the edges with a cellulose filler, so that the rock appears to be protruding from the ground and not stuck on top. As purchased, the bark is in pieces about 200mm × 100mm (8in × 4in) in size and often needs cutting into smaller pieces for use. As far as possible I use the natural weak points on the bark to break it up.

Once the bark is in place thought must be given as to how to turn its natural brown colour to something close to the colour of the rocks in the area being modelled. A thick coating of paint will destroy the colour variations in the bark and lose the realism—a very thin coat will have little effect. Two or more thin coats are a good idea as the end result can be approached with caution and that is my usual method. I have used both grey powder

paint and thinned down enamel paint and found that they have slightly different effects. The enamel paint soaks in and affects the whole surface equally, whereas the water in the powder paint tends to run off the surface and collect in the crevices, affecting those parts more than others. It is worth experimenting on a spare piece of bark to see which method creates the desired effect.

The final operation is laying the grass and foliage. Most visible rock outcrops are on open hillside surrounded by rough grass and bracken and with few trees and bushes close by. Less obvious outcrops do exist, of course, but not many modellers will want to make the effort to produce a rock outcrop in this way, and then to hide it behind a clump of trees or similar. Because of the age of the outcrops, most crevices will hold enough soil for a few tufts of grass, so when treating the area with whatever is used to represent grass, not only should it go all around the cork bark, but also in the crevices and other places on the bark itself. I generally make it a rule that most horizontal surfaces on the bark will have a bit of grass somewhere. Besides being prototypical, this helps the bark blend in more with the grass around it and look like part of the landscape.

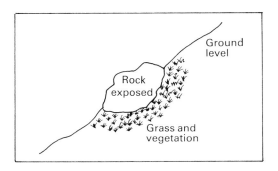

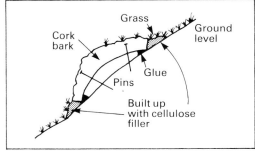

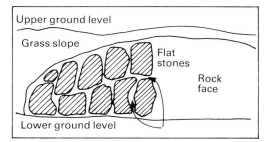

Upper ground level

Grass slope

Flat stones

Rock face

Lower ground level

Real Stone

There is an endless variety, both in colour and shape, of gravel and stones, and lumps of rock, shale and slate, that can be collected by the modeller and a considerable degree of selectivity must be employed to utilise only the pieces which blend well together. The ideal situation would be to collect enough pieces of stone from the area in which the model is based, but this is not always possible and substitutes often have to be sought. The rock faces of both my quarries are made of real slate slab from a prototype quarry close to the site of the fictitious model ones, but anyone who has tried to break up lumps of granite will be aware that not all types of stone will break up into pieces suitable for model use. Also, if there is any alternative, nobody will wish to make a special journey to a suitable site just to collect some lumps of rock.

When selecting pieces of stone for our purpose, we must consider the type of rock face in which it is to serve. For sheer faces, such as those that are found in quarries and railway cuttings, and also the cliff faces found both on the coast and inland in mountainous regions, the layered type of rocks such as shale and slate are most suitable, as they can be broken into pieces which are relatively thin in comparison to their length and breadth. For the type of rock face where large boulders are much in evidence, such as around mountain streams, three dimensional pieces will be required, and while layered rocks are still suitable if not made too thin, other stones can be collected from the garden, beach, gravel pile and so on, taking care to keep the colour variation to a minimum. Colour similarity is important in the chosen pieces of stone since painting the stone is a very poor second to using the natural colour. Painted stone always seems 'dead' as the paint takes away the natural reflective nature of the stone in varying light conditions.

If we select a stone which is fairly soft, such as shale, we will find that it is easy to break and shape. One of the coal mines near to where I live (Tilmanstone, East Kent) deposits as waste a dark grey shale which closely matches the slate from

the area on which my model is based, others have used shale from the North Cornwall coast to represent slate quarries also, so there is plenty of scope. Having selected our stone, we can turn to constructing the rock face. As methods differ somewhat between the sheer rock faces (quarries, cliffs, etc,); loose rock (slate tips, scree, etc) and rock river banks, I will deal with the three separately.

With cliffs, quarries and railway cuttings, the general shape will need to be formed and a solid base made prior to constructing the actual rock faces. This framework need only be roughly the shape required, but should be solid enough to support the weight of stone without sagging (I use hardboard). I have found that the best effect seems to be created if most of the stone pieces are fairly uniform in size, about 50mm × 35mm, with odd small pieces to fill the gaps.

To fix the stone to the framework we have built and fill the gaps between each stone, a cellulose filler (eg, Polyfilla) is the most suitable material I have found. The filler powder, which is usually white, needs to be mixed with powder paints until the colour matches that desired, black will be the predominant colour, with browns, blues, etc, to obtain the final shade. All this must be done dry, the mix darkens considerably as soon as water is

The 200 degree curve required at the end of the layout is realistically disguised by high ground, together with road overbridges to the right of this view. The large rock outcrop is a combination of cork bark and gravel in filler but would have been better completely modelled in cork bark, the author now feels.

A view over the top of the quarry showing how the raised ground separates different areas of the layout giving an appearance of greater distance. Note the neatly modelled cattle grid, road signs and fencing. Real rock has been used to model the rock faces in the quarry.

added. As the addition of powder paint weakens the filler, I mix in a quantity of PVA glue; this not only restores the strength but makes the finished product less likely to crack.

The filler is mixed to a fairly stiff consistency and spread over the area of the rock face. Immediately this is done, the stone pieces are pressed into the filler as close together as practial and with sufficient pressure to force the filler out through the gaps between the stones. If the filler sticks out too far, do nothing at this stage, but wait for a couple of hours until the filler has partly dried and use a small knife or scraper to remove the surplus. Once the filler is completely dry, and the stones firmly embedded, the surface can be touched up with emery cloth. Inevitably, there will be filler on the face of some of the stones and that between

the stones will be much darker than the colour that was mixed when dry. A rub with the emery cloth will remove the former and restore the surface of the latter to the desired colour, while leaving crevices and hollows darker assisting the illusion of depth.

The final task is the greenery. Grass will grow tight to the top of the rock face and usually just over the top, but it will depend on the nature of the rock and length of time the face has been exposed, whether there is grass growing on the face or at the foot, so think about the impression you are trying to create.

Exposed rock in the vicinity of rivers and streams varies widely from a few smallish boulders in the middle of a grassy banked stream, to a steep rocky gorge with a wildly corkscrewing tor-

Fig 6 First stage of the river bed, embedding stones into filler at the foot of the bank.

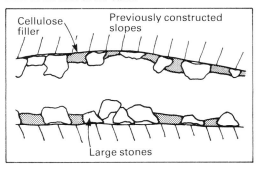

Fig 7 Completion of the river bed, glueing stones in place in the river itself.

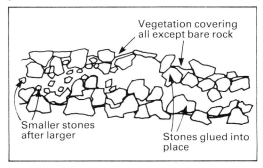

rent at the bottom. Where there is a gorge, the techniques for making the faces are similar to those described above, the method described here is mainly for dealing with the rockwork at river level.

As stated before, stones of a more three dimensional shape are needed here, either rounded or irregular, and a lot of them; a 1-2m long river could use up to 500 small stones. Having first built our river banks to the basic shape required (leaving them ungrassed) and constructed any rock faces by the method described above, we are ready to introduce the rockwork to the river bed and banks.

The edges of the stream and foot of the banks are the first to be dealt with using a mixture of the larger (15-20mm) and medium (10-15mm) size stones embedded in a layer of cellulose filler mixed as described previously. This enables the bank to be built up around the stones to give the impression of the rocks projecting from the main river bank profile. Once the filler has dried and the surface colour rubbed off with emery cloth, the stones can be placed in the river bed proper, between the rows of stones forming the banks. Starting with the largest, move along the river bed, gluing each stone down individually in the desired place, then do the same with the medium size stones, and finally, with the small ones. If a very rocky stream is required, this method is laborious but necessary, since just dropping the stones in at random does not create a very realistic effect. Once satisfied with the positioning of the stones, and with the glue properly dried out, cover the bed of the river with fine gravel (about the size of coarse '0' gauge ballast or budgie grit). This need not be stuck down, as the actual river material (varnish, casting resin etc,) will retain it, but care should be taken to only get the small gravel where it would realistically be expected. Alternatively, if varnish is used for the river, this gravel may be laid on the bed after the first layer of varnish has been laid and while it is still wet; this is the method that I use.

Grassing should not take place until the actual river is completed and should be carried out as required for the situation; unrealistic rocks can usually be hidden successfully beneath grass or a bush, so do not worry if everything does not appear perfect.

With scree, slate tips, etc, the basic shape of the hillside or tip should be formed beforehand and then small pieces of slate or shale, or fine gravel, glued on. For a slate tip, the pieces should be 6 to 12mm in size (with much smaller bits for the top surface), but the rock on a scree slope varies from small rubble to quite large rocks, all of which look as though they are about to continue their slide. As long as some with the correct colouring can be found, soft shale is most ideal for both tips and scree slopes, and once again it is better to lay the stones individually starting from the bottom and working upwards.

Vegetation will be non-existent on a slate or stone tip, and sparse on a scree slope, but once again it is important to work up the surrounding vegetation to unite the feature with the rest of the landscape.

When modelling in an area not normally considered rocky, railway cuttings and quarry workings often expose the underlying rock which may be some way below the surface. The exposed rock may be solid and hard (in which case it is best modelled by one of the other methods described) or else soft and crumbly, or have a high earth content, in which case I use the method described here.

The size of gravel that I use is about 2 or 3mm, budgie grit is suitable, although I also have a large lump of hard cement which can be broken up with a hammer and the bits graded to various sizes. Colour is not too critical as there is some scope for modifying the overall colour and reducing variations when the face is completed. The cellulose filler is mixed with powder paint and PVA glue as described previously, but as there is no opportunity to modify the surface colour by rubbing with emery cloth, the dry mix should be made lighter than the desired final effect. Alternatively, if suitable colours are available, a little emulsion paint can be used to tint the filler powder, this has the advantage of not reducing the strength as much as powder paint.

Now for the messy part. The fairly stiff mix of filler, paint, glue and water is spread thinly over the surface of the exposed face and immediately, handfuls of the gravel pressed into it, repeating this until the layer of filler is virtually covered with the bits of gravel stuck to it. A lot of gravel will have gone elsewhere but this can be removed once the filler on the rockface has dried, as can any loose bits of gravel on the face itself. Once dry, the colour of the rock face can be assessed and evened out by a little judicious touching up and/or an all over coat of thinned down powder or enamel paint. I have found that some colour variation in stones on a rock face of this kind does not look out of place.

Most rock faces of this type will have much more vegetation growing actually on the face than previous types, and in many cases will be more than half covered. If the filler is taken to be the earth, and the gravel taken as the rock, areas of bare filler can be covered with grass and foliage.

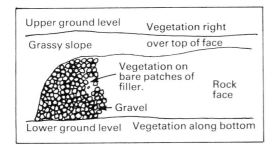

| Upper ground level | Vegetation right |
| Grassy slope | over top of face |

Vegetation on bare patches of filler.

Rock face

Gravel

| Lower ground level | Vegetation along bottom |

Left *Fig 8* Use of gravel and cellulose filler for rock faces.

Usually the vegetation overlaps the top and encroaches at the edges quite considerably. The fact that many of this type of rock face are sloping rather than vertical (more stable) also encourages growth of vegetation. Chalk cuttings (but not cliffs) are also ideal by this method (not too much of a colour problem either), and it can be used for loose scree, with small pieces of slate or shale in place of the gravel.

Sculptured modelling compound

This material, which includes Das, Pyruma and Pecoscene is a malleable compound which becomes hard when exposed to the atmosphere for a period of time. While undoubtedly most suitable for such things as stone buildings and walls etc, where there is a relatively even pattern

to be impressed onto a fairly flat surface, this material also has value in the modelling of rock faces, since it can be worked easily, will retain its shape while hardening and is quite strong when hard.

Again, a firm base is made and is wetted slightly to enable the compound to stick to the base when spread over it. After spreading to a suitable thickness over the whole area, the compound may be fashioned by suitable implements such as knife, spatula, scriber etc, which should be kept wet to avoid sticking to the compound. As the compound tends to 'drag' when the implements are drawn across its surface, this should be avoided wherever possible, and the fashioning done by pressing into the surface. When doing this, do try to have photographs of suitable prototype rock surfaces in front of you to work from. There is no amount of words that I can write which will say as much about how to shape a rock face as a few photographs.

As far as I know, there is no way of modifying the colour of the compound before application, so it will have to be painted after it has gone hard. The compound dries to a light stone colour, which is a good start, and is probably best treated

Llanymawddwy locomotive yard with the stream running into the lake. Note the realistic reflections and the weed and the slime at the edge of the lake. (Photograph by R. Wyatt).

An attractive view of Llanymawd-
dwy station showing the realistic
contours of the scenery. The rock
outcrops to the left of the retaining
wall and at the right of the picture
behind the train were modelled with
cork bark. Himalaya *climbs along-*
side the river with a train of loaded
wagons while Earl *shunts in the*
station yard. The campers beside
the river remind us that this is a
popular tourist area. Note the slate
fencing and the cattle grid to
prevent animals straying onto the
track.

from then on with a series of thin colour washes, gradually changing the colour to that required. Small areas can have a heavier coat of paint if so desired. Because this material has a stone like texture, it can be made into extremely realistic rock faces with careful painting. It is far easier to use than cellulose filler, but due to its relatively high cost in comparison with other methods, is best suited to fairly small areas.

Sculptured plaster or cellulose filler

Polyfilla and all its equivalents, is the main material here, but I would imagine a material such as Artex would be at least as good, although I have never used it. In this case, the extra strength required precludes the mixing with more than a small quantity of powder paint before application, although emulsion paint and PVA glue can be added. In this case, the final appearance of the rock face will depend much on the skill in painting once the material is dry, so at this stage it is sufficient just to remove the whiteness of the powder and so prevent any chips and scratches on the finished face becoming too glaring.

A fairly stiff mix is spread to the required thickness over a suitable framework which should be damp to promote adhesion. Do not spread too large an area at once, as cellulose fillers have a very limited time before they become unworkable. Tools should be anything which can be used in comfort, and will enable the desired effect to be created; I have even used a spoon handle. Efforts should be made to give some level of uniformity in the rock face, such as direction of strata, angles of cracks and crevices and so on, and with

experience it will be found that different features are best modelled at different stages of drying. When the mix is first applied, the whole area should be shaped roughly, probably with a spatula or similar; detail work at this stage will tend to round off and crevices will run together. As drying commences and the mix reaches the stage where it will retain whatever shape it is given, the outcrops, crevices and jagged edges can be worked in; until finally, as the filler becomes less workable and more crumbly, a scriber can be used to carve cracks etc, and produce small indentations. Do not worry about loose bits of filler at this stage, when the whole face is completed and dried hard, it may be brushed vigorously with a suede brush or similar. This will roughen the texture and remove the loose and most fragile bits, giving the face a weathered look.

For painting, thin washes of several different shades should be used, coating different parts of the face with each and without waiting for one coat to dry before applying the next, thus allowing different shades to blend together. Avoid too thick a coat of paint as this destroys the appearance of the rock material. If the rock face is stratified, a slight change of colour from one layer to the next is a good idea. The whole face can be made lighter or darker with an overall colour wash (remember that darkening is better as paint tends to collect in cracks and hollows which naturally look darker). Before, between or after the thin colour washes, consider applying a few streaks of almost dry paint to vary the effect. To obtain a realistic finish is clearly not easy and I would recommend that a complete dummy run is carried out and experience gained with different blends of colours until you are satisfied with your skill.

Sculptured polystyrene

I have had no experience of this method, but include it to complete the record, as I have seen it on some model railways and it can be effective. Polystyrene blocks are used and either broken or carved to give the required shape. When broken, this is done before installing on the layout, and the irregular, crumbly face that is left is reasonably suitable for the softer type of rock face, and also weathered outcrops. If the polystyrene is to be carved, the blocks are installed in the required position on the layout, allowing for the material that is going to be removed, and then carved with a knife or similar implement, heated as hot as is reasonably possible. In this way, the blade will melt its way through the polystyrene, preventing the crumbling that normally occurs.

Having carved and shaped the rock face, painting will give it realism; rather thicker coats of paint will be necessary with this material as it is rather porous and the paint will need to reach every nook and cranny. Once again, the face should be a blend of various shades, all applied while the previous coats are still wet, and once again, only experience will enable the necessary skills to be developed. In this case, however, it is easy to find suitable test pieces on which to practice.

It is clear from the foregoing that no single method will produce satisfactory results for every kind of rock face, so before selecting a suitable technique, consideration must be given as to what is to be reproduced. Where two totally different types of rock face are to be modelled (eg, weathered outcrops and a quarry face) two methods can be used on the same layout. Real stone can be used with sculptured cellulose filler on the same face, but indiscriminate mixing of methods and materials is not a good idea. Apart from those described here, there will be other ways of reproducing rock faces, but I hope the above will be of some help. The important thing is to do what you enjoy doing, after all, the hobby is meant to be a source of pleasure and satisfaction.

Foxes Farmhouse

Andy McMillan

Foxes Farmhouse is a set piece with which I am particularly and unashamedly pleased. This is probably because many people have rated it as amongst my best work, but then when many thousands of people have seen your work on permanent public exhibition, some are bound to enthuse. On the other hand, some give it the greatest snub by glancing at it as they pass and walking on to look at something more interesting to them. However, for those of you that have (or do) find it worth a second glance I shall attempt to explain the concept, confines and opportunities that created it.

The area is at one end of over 1,000 sq ft of model railway, which stretches away for 70ft into the distance. Six tracks had to be arranged to turn back on themselves and the eye had to be led into the layout from this, the first viewing point. Some sort of statement also had to be made visually so as to set the scene for the rest of the layout.

That old favourite 'the hill with tunnels' was chosen, mainly because it provided the bulk necessary to entice the eye down the valley into the rest of the layout. Allowing room for a station by making a cliff edge, gave an area of about two feet at the front, widening to nearly three further back, with a depth of some eight feet. A door and observation window for the operating staff intruded into the left hand wall and these had to be camouflaged as sky although unfortunately there did need to be a spy hole in the sky! The area was carefully considered and the need to make

visual impact demanded a small community of some sort. To lead the eye inwards a road was made leading from the front to curve out of sight and so arrest progress half way back. A side road was curved invitingly off to the left towards the wall to allow for access to something or other and the shell of the scenery constructed and given a good coat of plaster. As a public exhibition it was decided that colourful trains were needed and so the clock was set around the First World War period when railway traffic was at its peak and the colourful liveries of the pre-grouping companies offered many attractive variations of form and colour.

A rutted country lane was made and horses and carts became the featured transport. The cutting and tunnel mouth were created and the railway boundaries established. Between them and the lane a once large field had been chopped away to leave little more than an odd corner, so a marvellous opportunity for a farmyard dump presented itself and this was duly constructed from a number of kits and a variety of bits and bobs from the scrap box. Several major items are represented faithfully to show the nature of the dump, but over half of the models are just indistinguishable items of junk. Even the front buffer beam and framing from a broken Fleischman loco is in there somewhere! These create bulk and the progression from usable items at the front, through derelict but recognisable items to a nondescript heap at the back gives age and presence to the scene.

The overall scene described in this chapter breaks many of the conventinal modelling rules but looks nonetheless real for that. Foxes Farmhouse dominates the scene with firm severity, softened by the woodland surroundings and friendly warmth of the thatched cottages. The barn and neglected implements make for a cohesiveness that says 'Here is the heart of Old England'. (A. J. McMillan).

Left *The hill top rolls over out of sight with smaller trees and hedges on the right hand side to suggest far more depth than is really there. The windmill is a likely candidate for such a spot, giving another focal point amongst the trees, which themselves form a different angle, baffle the eye and frame the viaduct at the front right* (A. J. McMillan).

Farmyard junk, of course, needs a farmhouse close by, so Foxes Farmhouse was born. Always impressed by the Superquick model of such a building the basic shape and construction was expanded in the design modelled. The sizes and purposes of rooms behind the windows were considered and measured to provide for feasible living accommodation. The dining room is behind the bay window, a study next to it and a wide entrance hall behind the door. To the left is the drawing room stretching from front to back, the master bedroom above it. Other bedrooms occupy the rest of the top floor, with an attic window suggesting a garrett room at the right hand end. The slate hung end wall protects the house from driving rain blowing up the valley and over the stout hedge and bank rising from the lane. Being built on a slope, the house, I am sure, has cellars and access is no doubt gained from the scullery at a lower level to the right of the house. An extension beyond offers a huge farmhouse kitchen and further storage for food and supplies.

One would expect the house to be cut off during winter snows. It also gives necessary depth and helps the feeling of historic solidity that the building is intended to convey. A pile of logs, a wheelbarrow and a few tools show signs of life in this area. Perhaps I should have opened a bedroom window or two to help with that aspect! However, the front door is open and the milkman is probably having a 'cuppa' with the farmer's wife on his way back to the dairy. The farmer stands on the doorstep discussing a late lambing with the head shepherd. Their respective dogs are more interested in each other than the farm mouser, sensibly well out of reach by the rustic fencing, but near enough to show he's not too worried by their presence. The horse should have a nosebag, but his head is at the wrong angle. I never was any good at remodelling animals. The maid strides across the lane with sops for the pigs. They shouldn't be quite so close to a gentleman farmer's house of course and they could push their way under that barbed wire whenever they

Left *Here the viaduct is the focal point because of its size. To prevent the eye wandering away, the upwards sweep of the valley side leads the eye first to the tunnel mouth, then up along the line of trees and back down the centre of the valley to the viaduct again* (A. J. McMillan).

Right *Front view from above the lane shows the depth of the model. The cottages and further hills help to suggest room to move about in the hamlet. The farming community is surrounded by its farm* (A. J. McMillan).

Right *Detail of farmer's junk pile* (A. J. McMillan).

Right *Detail of farmer's junk pile* (A. J. McMillan).

felt like it, but nobody produced a convincing mare and foal at the time the model was made and she had to be going to feed something! I have so often gone to great lengths to model something only to find it available commercially shortly after it's finished. So on larger layouts where there is often a time span of several years from inception to completion, it is often worth putting in something commercially available that is right in spirit but wrong in detail to complete the scene, so that if something better comes along later it can be substituted. If not, one just has to get one and make it properly, but at least the model looks finished in the meanwhile. Incidentally, there is a battered iron mink with replacement wooden doors and a window set up on wooden bolsters in one corner of the pen with straw and other rough

detail in and around its musty interior, but the cameraman obviously thought it too ugly to photograph. The trees on the left form a highly suitable frame to this side of the picture, and incidentally prevent the gated lane, which is created in the inch and a half between the gate and the backscene, from being seen at the wrong angle thus destroying the illusion. Seen from another angle this lane appears to lead through the woods to further fields thus making the end of the layout much less obvious.

No farm is complete without a barn and this is a large timber structure a few yards up the lane. Its gaping doors admit precious little light to its musty interior but its well worn approach suggests more use than might otherwise be assumed. Heaven only knows what goodies lay mouldering inside, but wouldn't you just love to wander in and look around! The thousands of individually cut, coloured and affixed tiles on that roof were fitted by one of the staff called Sheila. She has since married and gone to study wildlife in Africa. It no doubt takes less patience!

Gentleman farmers were often the turn of the century equivalent of farm managers. Their forebears had built up the farms and made the family estates and no doubt many of the farm hands were older than the farmer, but nowhere near as old as their tithe cottages. These ancient thatched varieties of the kind now much sought after as country retreats by city folk make fascinating models in themselves but here are simply an excuse for some bright colour in both themselves and their gardens. Beehives may just be discernible in the farthest garden while the tree bordered lane curves out of sight, again to the right, so as to take the eye away from the wall and into the model. The continuation of the lane above the cottages rolls over the hill top as do the fields and

Left *This view from along the layout shows well the lane in the back-scene, but note that while the farmhouse is still visible, it is partly obscured and thus loses in relative importance. The bright cottages are completely hidden behind the trees and so the whole scene becomes a background to the train* (A. J. McMillan).

Below left *This barn must be 200 years old and probably took at least two days to build!* (A. J. McMillan).

hedgerows, while a shaped piece of card suggests a building on the distant horizon.

All of these items, from and including the cottages to the back of the model, are built in perspective. Trees and other buildings hide most of the wrong angle so that this is not immediately apparent and, in fact, the photographs show up the perspective better than actually looking at the model.

There is a great deal of lush vegetation around the scene, something over two hundred trees, mainly of the 'bottle brush' type but some white metal and twig trunks are to be seen, dead heather

collected on holidays in wild moorlands being particularly effective en masse when suitably foliated. I would have liked to model other details such as a tethered goat in the junkyard field. Perhaps greater attention to the flower beds in the farmhouse front garden would have improved things but then the whole scene is some 20 sq ft out of a thousand or more and time is never unlimited. With the various criticisms noted above taken into account (and no doubt you can add some of your own), I am still extremely pleased with the results of this area and the fact that it is finished and stands as a model in its own right while still forming part of a larger scene. Hopefully this gives credence to my theory of breaking the model into visual chunks which can be enjoyed one at a time. Like the separate courses of a formal dinner, each one should be a delight in its own right, but complementary to the whole of the feast!

My own particular pleasure in model making is to see the reactions of people who have never seen anything like it before. There is the added enjoyment of the creating, of seeing your model grow from care, patience and cardboard into a model, but the collection of models to form a scene, the collection of scenes to form a landscape the whole of which tells a story is all the more enjoyable when other people get pleasure from seeing it too. I work from two pieces of excellent advice. The first, from Allan Downes, was to 'take a piece of card and a Stanley and make a start', while the other was from Mr Beeson who is quoted as saying, 'Finish the model'. What more can I add?

Low relief modelling

Bob Petch

The art of the modeller is in creating a life like railway in miniature and the whole scene must have an overall perspective. To achieve realism we want to avoid a sudden end to the scenery at the back of the model. Instead we need a convenient limit to the layout which will not only help to guide the eye towards the focal point of the scene, usually the station complex, but will also give the illusion of the scenery extending into the distance.

One means of accomplishing this is the installation of a painted or printed backscene. However, most modellers have no training in art and will find it difficult to paint a convincing scenic background. The commercial backdrops are expertly produced but may not be appropriate to the modelled scenery. They also have the disadvantage of appearing frequently on other layouts and thus lose some of their effectiveness. And, though skilfully designed, they are of course only two dimensional with no actual depth.

A great improvement in appearance and realism can be achieved by the use of low relief models to form a transition between the fully modelled scenery in front and a flat background behind. Such low relief structures have only a front, together with the front parts of the sides and roof. They are thus much easier and quicker

Fig 1 A simple low relief model.

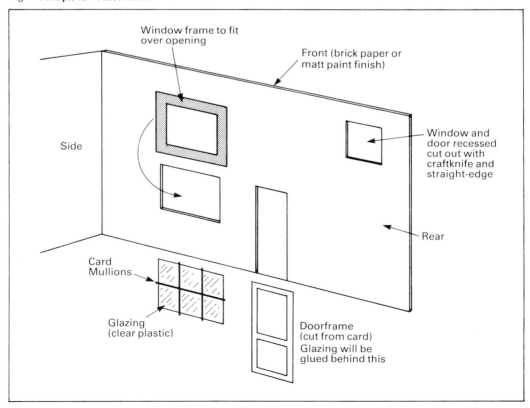

Window frame to fit over opening

Front (brick paper or matt paint finish)

Side

Window and door recessed cut out with craftknife and straight-edge

Rear

Card Mullions

Glazing (clear plastic)

Doorframe (cut from card) Glazing will be glued behind this

Left and below left *These two views of the low relief models at Shepton Gurney show how well they link the fully modelled foreground with the painted backscene giving the impression of a busy town street and adding greatly to the realism, interest and effect of depth.*

to construct than normal fully modelled buildings. However, because the facades are modelled with glazed window recesses, raised window sills, doorsteps, and perhaps porches, awnings or other protruding details, they do actually have some depth and the effect is much more realistic than a flat painted reproduction would be. As the models are at the rear of the scene or layout less detail is necessary than for models at the front. Behind the low relief structures we need only a simple sky background, though the addition of a few flat cut outs of trees or other buildings will give the impression of features behind the low relief models and will enhance the impression of depth. These flats can be cut from commercial backscenes or can be drawn and painted by the modeller as only a simple representation is required.

As always in modelling scenery or structures you should do some planning beforehand, deciding in advance the best positions and relationships to create the overall result you want. You can try different buildings in various positions to produce the best visual effect. If you use simple mock-ups from card you can even do this

before you have constructed the buildings. You may find that such experimentation will lead you to make changes in the size or shape of some of the structures you then model. Choosing buildings of different sizes, shapes and styles will add variety. In general you are best to model a number of small or moderate sized structures rather than one large building as this not only gives more variety but also gives the impression of a larger area.

There are a number of kits available for low relief structures and ordinary kits can easily be modified. An advantage is that the front and rear of a single kit can often be used for two separate low relief models thus saving on costs. Modifications of the kits with details and parts from other kits will help to alter the appearances and add extra variety and interest. Low relief models can also be scratchbuilt of course and, as previously indicated, are easy and quick to construct. Whenever possible base your models on real buildings, even if you modify them considerably, as this helps to give authenticity to the scene.

You can add variety by leaving gaps between some buildings filled in by a fence or wall perhaps with trees behind. An archway into a courtyard or an ancient stone gateway, as shown in the photographs, can also break up the rows of structures to good effect. The impression of depth can be enhanced by having some of the buildings extend slightly further forwards than others.

Mounting groups of structures together on bases can be very convenient for construction and installation, and for removal for maintenance and repairs. The bases can include the pavement complete with figures, lamp posts, and other details if you wish. Interior detailing is often unnecessary as the models are in the background but curtains at the windows and merchandise in shop windows are worth adding as they are easily visible. A final touch that can be added if you wish is interior lighting following the usual

The left hand end of the street showing, from the left, the pub (1), cinema (2), restaurant (3), offices (4), pub 'The Daniel Gooch' (5) and the bookshop (6). Note how a fully modelled structure has been used to partly mask the end of the street and the junction with the painted scene.

principles for conventional buildings.

Perhaps I can best describe how to tackle the modelling of low relief street scenes by relating my own experiences with my layout, 'Shepton Gurney'. I believe that excellent results can be achieved with a compromise of kits and scratch-built structures. Some years ago when I assembled my first layout I used Superquick kits for speed and convenience and I soon found them to be ideal for modifying and using along with scratch built models. Superquick also produce brick papers for this purpose so it is really quite easy to construct a street of varied buildings all in the same style. However, the scene is more interesting if the shops, inns, cinemas, pubs and banks are varied in shape, design and style.

My layout, 'Shepton Gurney', is situated in the loft and as the house is semi-detached with a party wall through the loft I decided to place the townscape at this end where headroom is at maximum. This decision proved quite a challenge

as I then had 14 feet of street scene to contend with. So, like all good town planners, I turned to the drawing board and set about designing the street, choosing the kind of buildings I required and deciding how the street could 'disappear' into the backscene. I also considered how I could employ existing structures and models rescued from my previous layouts.

Let's have a look at Station Road, Shepton Gurney, starting from the left hand side of the layout. I will describe each structure in general and then concentrate on the detailed construction of the largest building, the Dolphin hotel.

1 Pub Part of a Superquick low relief kit, plus a card wall to join the cinema. You can easily adapt these excellent kits and use parts of them in different places.

2 Cinema Builder Plus kit with card sections added to give more depth.

3 Restaurant and **4 Offices** A Superquick low relief kit which makes up into three buildings. I

Passing further along the street we see from left the Dolphin Hotel (7), Lloyds Bank (8), the baker (9), the solicitor's office (10) and the archway (11).

This view shows, from left, the baker's shop (9) with a delivery boy and his bicycle outside, the solicitor's office (10), the archway (11), a newsagent (12) and a drapery shop (13). The archway is used to conceal the fact that the street passing back through it has to stop almost immediately as it reaches the backscene.

separated the pub (used as **1**) and combined the restaurant and Norwich Union offices with the pub in **5**.

5 Pub Every Station Road has to have its railway pub and this one is called 'The Daniel Gooch'. The building was scratchbuilt from card, with the doors and windows carefully cut out with a craft knife. The saloon bar windows were formed in the shape of carriage windows. Drink advertisements from the Tiny Signs range were added to the facade.

6 Bookshop Scratchbuilt and covered with brickpaper. Having cut out the window space and glazed it I had great fun in making small shelves and filling them with books made from scraps of

thin card and paper glued together. The shop has a canopy extending over the pavement; this was made from a piece of material glued to a frame made up from plastic micro strip.

7 The Dolphin Hotel This is a rather special structure and is described in more detail below.

8 Lloyds Bank Scratchbuilt from card using the same method as for the pub **5**. It was based on a model on Peter Denny's 'Buckingham Great Central' layout. The windows are of the sash type and it is fairly simple to model some of these in an open position.

9 Baker's This small scratch built facade is covered with Superquick brick paper. Inside the shop window are dozens of loaves cut from balsa.

To the right of the archway are, from left, the newsagent (12), the drapery shop (13), a chemist (14) and an antique shop (15),

Proceeding to the right from the antique shop (15) at the left of this picture we pass the post office (16), bank (17) and estate agent (18).

The low relief scene is completed by the section of old castle wall (19) and the warehouse (20). Note how the warehouse has been positioned at an angle to the backscene to help lead into the corner realistically.

The delivery boys help to bring some life to the street scene. This shop also has an extending canvas canopy represented by stretched tissue material.

10 Solicitor's office Scratchbuilt from card and painted with emulsion. The window sills and lintels are cut from obeche and painted in a lighter colour. All downpipes are made from plastic rodding.

11 The Archway This structure is based on an ancient gateway in my home city, through which the trams used to rattle. The model is made from Peco embossed plastic card and glued to hardboard for strength. I first drew a plan of the gateway's approximate dimensions based on photographs and site studies. The structure is of key importance to the layout for two reasons. Firstly it provides a link between the two stretches of street scene and a focal point of interest in the background to the layout. Secondly it allows the street and tramway to 'disappear' into the backscene. Careful planning and painting of the backscene helped to keep that all important perspective in proportion.

12 Newsagent Scratchbuilt from card again using brick paper and grey slate roofing paper to good effect.

13 Drapery shop Scratchbuilt again, inspired by a feature in a modelling magazine. The rounded windows have a certain appeal and can be simply made using thin and flexible transparent plastic. Small offcuts of material, coloured tissues and paper were used to model the window displays.

14 Chemist Scratchbuilt using embossed stone card. There is a second entrance at the front of the building to gain access to the insurance office above the chemist shop.

15 Antique shop This is a similar structure with an office above the shop. Window sills are cut from thick card and lintels from cartridge paper, glued in place after painting. This shop also has a canopy and the windows are crammed full of antiques and advertisements.

16 Post Office Essential to every Station Road, this cut down Superquick kit blends in well with the scratchbuilt shops. Strategically placed downpipes help to cover any gaps between buildings when they are glued together.

17 Bank Another old Superquick faithful. It is quite common to have a bank next to a post office in a busy street. I used to work in such a bank and at least once a week someone would call in and ask for stamps or give me a parcel to weigh.

18 Estate Agent Superquick kit. I should point out here that to avoid the monotony of the street running parallel with the backscene the pavement widens from the Antique Shop onwards. This extra depth allows for a complete building to fit in, such as in 17 and 18, whilst all that was necessary with the Post Office was an extension to the roof to give it more depth.

19 Walls This is simply a section of old castle wall with an entrance to provide some interest. The wall is made from Peco embossed stone card in the same style as the Archway and the intention is to suggest that the castle wall runs along behind the shops. I love painting trees (it is far easier than modelling them.) so the backscene reflects the large trees inside the walls; possibly the castle grounds have ornate gardens? You'll have to scale the walls to find out.

20 Warehouse This is a scratchbuilt model, adapted from an Allan Downes article in a 1975 *Railway Modeller*. The building is cut from thick card, faced with Superquick stone paper, and has only three sides and a shallow roof. There is a loading bay constructed in the centre of the warehouse and a small winch protrudes from underneath the central eave. The small office is built in the same style and the yard is cluttered with every bit of scrap modelling material I could find. The roof is made from ¼in strips of fine wet and dry sandpaper nicked every ¼in and overlaid to give a very effective slate covering.

The Dolphin Hotel

The Dolphin Hotel is an attempt to recreate fairly accurately a stately building in my local High Street which was once a busy coaching inn. I started by taking a couple of photographs and also worked from postcards and site inspections. I then drew a front elevation on graph paper, of which I still have a quantity in the old Imperial sizes. My building ended up 12in long, 8in high and 2in deep. I was a little concerned that it might appear too prominent in a small townscape but modeller's licence says that just about anything goes, and you can be forgiven for a lot if the end result looks right.

I planned the construction in the following stages, using 2mm thick card. **1** The overall facade up to the eaves was cut out from a single piece of card (12in × 6¼in). The sides (2in × 6¼in) were also cut out at this time. **2** The lower part of the facade with the stucco effect was to be overlaid so a second piece of card was cut measuring 12in × 2¼in. **3** The central section of the facade above the entrance arch was to be slightly proud of the overall frontage so a further section of card (2¼in × 3½in) was cut for this. **4** The elegant bow windows in fine Georgian style were to be made as separate units and then glued to the facade. **5** The balcony. **6** The roof and dormer windows. **7** The crest.

I began by measuring the window recesses in item **3**, and after cutting these out I covered the whole with brick paper. It's a good idea to ensure that the glue is fairly evenly spread and when the paper is on squarely rest a couple of volumes of model railway magazines on top while it sets. The window frames and mullions were made from thick paper and glued in place behind the glazing which consists of any clear plastic I have available. Curtains were added last. I then put item **3** to one side.

Next came the lower front (item **2**) with the entrance arch. Again, the window positions and

Fig 2 Drawing of the Dolphin Hotel.

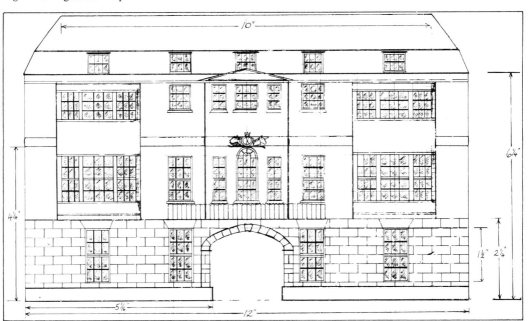

Views of the Dolphin Hotel model. The hotel has its own base modelled as pavement and cobbled drive complete with gas lamps and a group of pedestrians.

arch were marked and cut out using a craft knife and straight edge. The stucco effect was achieved by ruling lines across at 7mm intervals and then forming a brick pattern with 15mm intervals using a large ball point pen applied with pressure. This produced a very pleasing effect. The archway was then bordered by sections of 2mm card cut and glued on individually. A strip of card 1cm high was then glued to the bottom of the section. The sash windows were made in two sections, again cut from thick cartridge paper. The top window was glued in place and the second, lower, window fixed in position and recessed to allow for the top window to slide down.

I placed the two completed items over the main front section and marked the openings for windows and entrance to be cut out. In addition I marked and cut out the two windows either side of the central section and the large openings over which the bow windows would be placed. The main facade was then covered with brick paper and while the glue was drying I started measuring the card for the bow windows. These windows are semi-circular and are 3¾in high and 3¾in long when laid flat before shaping. I scribed four circles of 2¼in diameter and carefully cut out and then halved these. For each window three lengths of card were cut, ¼in, 1in and ½in strips all 3¾in long, and strips 5/16in and ⅛in wide for use as uprights. The three lengths which would form the framework of the bow were carefully pulled between finger and thumb to form a curved shape. When satisfied that they would retain this new shape I glued them to the semi-circular supports as shown in the drawing. This was followed by glueing the upright supports and clear perspex for the windows in place. The use of a good impact adhesive such as Evostick helps to secure the structure quickly and it can then be tested against the main facade. After adding the window frames and mullions of the Georgian windows I then finished the bow windows by adding micro-strip to the horizontal and vertical frames. Finally Letraset is used outwards one

A side view of the Dolphin Hotel showing its limited depth.

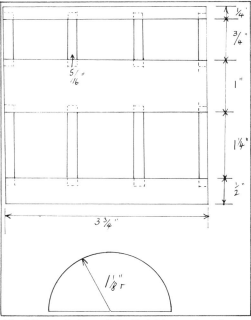

Fig 3 Bow window of the Dolphin — size of parts required.

letter at a time either side of the central letter, that is the P in Dolphin and the T in hotel. This ensures that the lettering is evenly spaced. A protective coat of Humbrol matt varnish was then applied.

At this stage items **2**, **3** and **4** were glued in place on the main facade, item **1**. The balcony measures 4½ in by ½ in and was cut from card, the railings being modified GWR station fencing. A long balsa trough was made to fit inside and various pieces of greenery and lichen were added to represent thriving window box plants. White downpipes were glued to the sides of the central facade and a moulding was added 4¼ in from the base.

On top of the facade a double thickness of card in a ⅜ in strip, covered with brick paper was overlaid and bordered by white micro-strip moulding. A central pointed eave was constructed from micro-strip and glued in place. All that remained was to glue on the sides so that the structure could stand upright, before turning to the roof and dormers.

The roof was made from ¼ in strips of paper, nicked with scissors every ¼ in and overlaid in rows to form tiles. When dry the whole roof was painted with poster paint, mostly red with black and brown added for weathering. The five dormers were cut into the roof with sides and window frames made from thin card and glazed in the usual way. The flat top to the roof was made

from a strip of card 1 in × 10¼ in and 2mm thick painted in poster colours to match.

The crest, which is the lion and unicorn badge with *'Dieu et mon droit'* inscribed around the centre, was made from scraps of card. The lion was modelled from a cut down Airfix sheepdog and the unicorn from a horse with a piece of thin plastic rod as the horn. The scene was completed with a pair of ornate gas lamps decorating the entrance. One can imagine the scene in the 19th century as the late night coach enters through the archway with hooves and wheels shattering the still of the cold, gas lit night. . .

So there we have it, 14ft of varied low relief modelling which has to blend into the layout. There are a few points that should be borne in mind as a conclusion if the scene is to achieve the desired objective of realism. Firstly, the backscene must line up with the low relief buildings. I use lengths of hardboard a foot wide and 8ft long painted with undercoat. The trees and hills, buildings and other features are then carefully drawn in and painted in poster colours. I paid a great deal of attention to the intended street scene beyond the archway by representing the perspective of distance. If you plan to have trees close to the backscene then try to represent similar trees on the scenic background. Secondly, buildings   tend   to   take   a   battering   from

A close up of the hotel front showing some of the details.

exhibitions and even more so from the extremes of temperature in a loft. Therefore spare no effort in strengthening the structures with thick card partition walls and floors and with bracing preferably of a hard wood such as obeche rather than balsa. I have learnt from experience that it pays to use an abundance of 11mm × 5mm obeche — it's amazing just how quickly a 2 metre length disappears.

Finally, bring life to the street scene by adding figures, pillar boxes and a telephone box, telegraph poles, gas lamps and, as in the case of Shepton Gurney, standard poles for the tramway. Next time you walk down your local high street take a closer look at the buildings, the architecture and the street furniture. Then apply your observations in your modelling. And notice also that for all you can see of the buildings apart from their facades they too could be low relief structures just as in your model street scene.

Canal modelling

Michael Andress

Any well modelled stretch of water can be a very striking scenic feature on a model railway layout, be it a lake, river, pond or even the sea. Apart from the interest it adds to the scene it can also provide an effective scenic break between different tracks and areas. Of the various types of water features we can choose to model a canal is particularly appropriate. There have always been close links between the railways and the canals; some of the railway companies operated their own boats and even owned some of the canals. Railway tracks and canals often run on parallel routes, or cross each other and there is interchange of cargo between them. Though sometimes rivals for trade, these links and the cooperation in transporting many goods and materials were of benefit to both.

There are many advantages for the railway modeller in incorporating a canal into the scenery of a layout. It adds another contrasting form of transport with opportunities to model the transfer of cargo from one to another. Canals are narrow and often run parallel to the railway which means that one can be fitted conveniently onto the layout even if the baseboard is narrow. If a short section of canal is all that is wanted or all that can be accommodated this can be realistically managed by arranging the canal so that it disappears into a tunnel or under a bridge. Unlike other forms of water which find the lowest part of the scene canals do not have to be at the most dependent point in the landscape. They may be low down, raised up with artificially formed

banks, or even carried on embankments or aqueducts over other features such as rivers or railway tracks. They can also change height with one or more locks and can be very flexible in fitting in with your requirements for the scene you are modelling.

Canals are equally appropriate in rural settings or built up areas with many industries. They have many features which can be modelled to provide extra interest and realism. Most characteristic are the locks. These are usually single but sometimes several are sited together as a staircase of locks where a greater change of level is required. Bridges will be needed where railways, roads and footpaths must cross the canal. Often these are plate girder bridges for railways and hump backed bridges for roads and footpaths. Occasionally

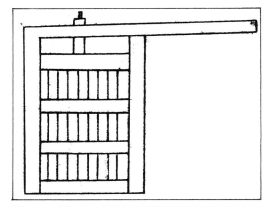

Right *This model Dutch canal at Legoland features boats moving through real water guided by underwater wires, and a working lifting bridge.*

Right *The famous aqueduct at Haverud in Sweden, carrying the canal over a river. Similar aqueducts are to be seen in Britain.*

Below left *Fig 1* Typical lock gate.

Bottom left *A delightful Dutch canal scene at Legoland; this large scale outdoor model uses real water in its canal system. The buildings, the canal boats and even the cows are modelled from Lego blocks.*

a drawbridge is seen, of the type more frequently built in Holland. An aqueduct carrying a canal over a river, railway or valley is an interesting feature and may take the form of a plate girder bridge or a brick or stone viaduct. A wide range of buildings are seen beside canals including cottages and houses (some built for the canal workers and lock keepers) inns, factories, warehouses and even stables for the many horses at one time employed in hauling the canal boats. Thus a canal can be an excellent addition to the scenery for a model railway layout not only because of its intrinsic appeal but also for the wide variety of interesting associated features which can be included if the modeller wishes.

Having looked briefly at the potential offered by canal modelling we can now consider the construction of such a feature for a layout. As always, for all forms of scenic modelling, careful planning is desirable before construction is

Below *The aqueduct at Haverud is featured in model form at Legoland. In this view a boat is seen crossing the aqueduct while a train passes over the bridge above both the river and the aqueduct. A working lock, just visible in the right foreground, completes the scene.*

Left *A beautifully modelled lock scene in 2mm scale on the 2mm Scale Association's layout. The lock, canal boats and canalside inn were all modelled from scratch. Note the details, including the life-belts on holders at each end of the lock.*

Centre left *A canal tunnel on an 00 scale layout under construction by Terry Jenkins. The canal tunnel mouth is typically smaller and simpler in style than the railway tunnel mouth beside it.*

Bottom left *Terry Jenkins modelled this canal scene in 00 scale for a small layout. Note the typical hump-backed road bridge built from scratch. The narrow boat was made up from a Novus colour printed card kit.*

Below *A small canal basin with loading crane, rail siding and ware-house building constructed in 00 scale by Terry Jenkins. The two canal boats were built from scratch.*

Right *An 00 scale canal under construction by Terry Jenkins. The stone siding for the canal and lock is Faller embossed card and the lock gates were built up from balsa.*

Right *An 00 scale canal under construction by Terry Jenkins. The stone siding for the canal and lock is Faller embossed card and the lock gates were built up from balsa.*

begun. Ideally the canal should be planned in connection with the track layout and the scenic design generally, so that it will fit realistically and appropriately into the landscape.

With the course of the canal decided, the baseboard and scenery supports will be arranged so that the canal is sunk below the level of the banks; allowance also being made for any changes in level introduced by locks. The width of the canal must be sufficient to allow two boats to pass, though the locks are often only wide enough for a single boat. Construction will vary slightly with the technique used to represent the water. A number of methods are employed in scenic modelling to simulate water but some are more suited to canal modelling than others. Perhaps I can first mention the use of real water, to largely dismiss it as unsuitable. It has been used successfully out of doors particularly with larger scale models enabling working model boats to be employed. A fine example is at the famous Legoland in Denmark where there is a considerable extent of model lake, sea, and canal all with real water and with model boats moved and guided by underwater cables. One scene based on the aque-

Above right *The canal on Mike Sharman's 4mm scale 19th century period layout has these two realistically modelled locks.*

Right *Mike Sharman has modelled the lower lock with both gates shut. Note the mooring bollards and the bird perched on one of the gates. The recessed areas to take the gates when open are well seen in this view.*

Left *The upper lock has a canal boat moving out through the open upper gates, which are swung back into the recesses. The narrow boat was scratchbuilt by Mike Sharman.*

Below *Fig 2* Typical construction methods.

duct at Haverud in Sweden actually includes an operating lock. However real water is not usually suitable for indoor layouts. It is heavy, likely to leak and evaporate, is easily spilt and can quickly become stagnant, dirty and smelly. And it is not as realistic as modelled water because it does not scale down.

There are two methods of representing water that are particularly suitable for canals. A cheap, convenient and effective way of modelling water is the paint and varnish method. Because the water in canals is usually fairly still we can use hardboard, smooth side uppermost, to model the water. The hardboard will be fitted at the appropriate level below the banks, properly supported to avoid warping, and painted a suitable colour depending on the depth of water, muddiness, and so on to be simulated. Usually a dark brown-green-blue blend is appropriate. This is allowed to dry. The banks are modelled with plaster for natural banks or with embossed plastic card for a brick or stone canal side at a factory wharf or basin. The banks are also painted and scenic dressings are applied as required. Then several coats of clear varnish (polyurethane is very suitable) are applied to the water allowing each to dry before the next is put on. This produces a shiny wet looking surface which is very realistic. A minor variation on the method described above is to use plaster for the water surface instead of the hardboard. The plaster is smoothed on and a spatula or the fingers are used to model ripples. The plaster is allowed to harden after which it is paint-

ed and varnished as with the hardboard. As an alternative to clear varnish the use of gloss acrylic medium used by artists to protect their pictures, is becoming popular, particularly in the United States. This is a thick white liquid which dries clear and hard in about half an hour. Colour can be added using acrylic paint if you wish. If a rippled surface is wanted the medium is applied, allowed to stiffen for 10 minutes or so and then brushed or stippled to produce the ripples.

The other main method is the use of clear casting plastic, a technique for modelling water first introduced in the United States and now becoming popular here. The plastic is the type sold in toy and craft shops for making paperweights and other items of clear plastic within which shells, flowers, etc, are embedded. The material comes as liquid plastic and separate hardener; these are mixed just before use in the proportion indicated in the instructions and the plastic is then allowed to harden. To use this method the canal bed is modelled with plaster and painted appropriately; the colours should be kept lighter than wanted for the final result as they will appear darker when the plastic is applied. There must be no gaps where the liquid plastic could leak out and if the canal comes to the edge of the baseboard the gap must be temporarily sealed off. This is easily done by glueing a piece of thick card or hardboard across the space. The layout must be level when the plastic is poured in; if not the water level will be sloping when the plastic has set and will not be realistic. Because the plastic has a strong and

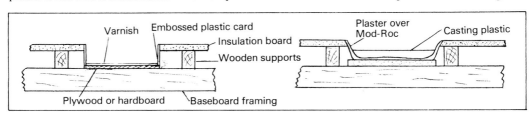

Two views of the canal on the Great Exmouth 00 Model Railway layout. Many interesting, detailed scenes, separate but linked by the canal, have been modelled along the banks.

A busy canal basin with loading and unloading taking place in the foreground, while behind this a holiday canal boat is seen in the main canal. Gerry Nicholson modelled this interesting scene for his Great Exmouth 00 Model Railway exhibition layout. The canal boats were built from Craftline Models kits.

rather irritant smell good ventilation is essential; if the weather is fine you may like to do the pouring outdoors. When preparations are complete the plastic is made up, poured in, and allowed to harden. Several layers are applied to add to the impression of depth given by the painting. Dyes are available to add colour to the plastic if desired and also enhance the appearance of depth. Extra hardener can be added to the plastic for the final layer; hardening then takes place more quickly and this causes a slight rippling of the top surface giving a realistic effect. The technique of modelling water with casting plastic is very effective but is more expensive than the paint and varnish method.

Most modellers will want to include at least one lock on their canal. Locks are fairly simple to model but add greatly to the interest. The lock can be modelled with the water level high or low with both gates closed or with one open and the other shut. It is probably best to model the lock with the water level low as this shows more of the lock walls and gates and looks more interesting to the viewer. The two levels for the base of the canal must be appropriately positioned and the walls of the lock, which are usually stone or brick, can be

modelled with embossed plastic card. Lock gates are available in kit form; Craftline Models have wood kits in 4mm scale while Langley Miniature Models make cast metal 'Waterways Scene' kits in 00 and N scales which include lock gates, motor and butty boats, bollards and figures. Alternatively lock gates can be modelled quite easily in wood or plastic card. The usual arrangement is to have a single gate at the upper end of the lock and a double gate at the lower, though often both are double. The single gate fits square across the lock but the double gates make a 'V' when closed. The gates should be painted a dark brown or black and can be touched up on their lower parts with some scenic dressing and green paint to represent slime and weed on the parts which are under water when the lock is full. The towing path will be provided with a ramp and steps for the change in height at the lock and these should be modelled. A lock keeper's cottage and perhaps a canalside inn, together with details such as bollards, a seat, a lifebelt on a board, and so on will complete the scene. The buildings can be constructed from card, wood or plastic card following the usual scratchbuilding techniques or can be appropriate or adapted kits.

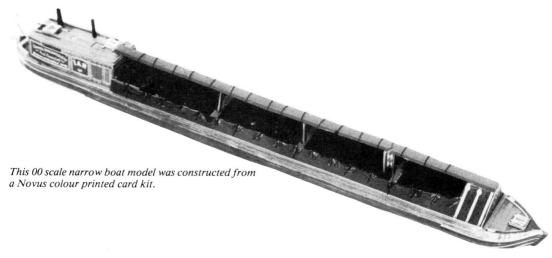

This 00 scale narrow boat model was constructed from a Novus colour printed card kit.

Above *Two models from the Craft-line Models range in 4mm scale. They are two 70-foot coal boats, a horse-drawn boat in front and a motor boat behind.*

Right *This photograph taken at Foxton locks shows details of typical lock gates. Note also the recessed sections to take the gates when they are open, the treads fixed to the ground to provide footholds for the men opening the gates, and the small bridge allowing pedestrian access across the lock.*

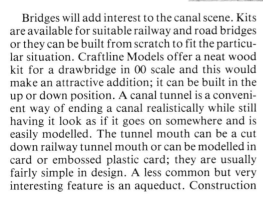

Bridges will add interest to the canal scene. Kits are available for suitable railway and road bridges or they can be built from scratch to fit the particular situation. Craftline Models offer a neat wood kit for a drawbridge in 00 scale and this would make an attractive addition; it can be built in the up or down position. A canal tunnel is a convenient way of ending a canal realistically while still having it look as if it goes on somewhere and is easily modelled. The tunnel mouth can be a cut down railway tunnel mouth or can be modelled in card or embossed plastic card; they are usually fairly simple in design. A less common but very interesting feature is an aqueduct. Construction must be justified by the contours of the landscape and will be similar to a railway plate girder bridge or viaduct.

There are many buildings to be found beside canals. These include cottages and houses, inns and warehouses. Often factories and other industrial premises such as brick works, timber yards, coal depots, quarries, sand and gravel works, and so on are served by canals. These can be very effective in model form and there are various kits which can be employed with or without modification to represent such industries. The wharf may merely be at the side of the canal or there may be a basin leading off the canal where boats can be

This 4mm scale barge loading facility was scratchbuilt from wood and plastic; it is closely based on the coal loader at British Oak Disposal Point, Crigglestone. The barge was built from wood and card following a Skinley drawing.

loaded and unloaded. Often there will be one or more cranes at such sites, usually hand operated cranes similar to goods yard cranes, or derricks. Suitable kits are available for both types in the Mikes Models range of cast metal kits. Additional details will include bollards and mooring posts, signs and notices, lifebelts, workmen, etc. Such items are available as accessories or can be modelled from odds and ends. Appropriate cargo should also be modelled.

The typical and best known canal boats are the narrow boats, originally horse drawn but later diesel powered, often with an unpowered butty trailing behind. Some of the canal boats have been converted to holiday cruisers. Models of powered, unpowered, and converted boats are all available in 00 scale as kits, and I believe also as made up models, from Craftline; construction is of wood with colour printed thin card for the painted panels. Cast metal kits are made by Langley Miniature Models in 00 and N scales for motor and butty boats. A card kit in 4mm scale was produced by Novus but I do not know if this is still on the market. For the scratchbuilder Skinley have 4mm scale drawings of a towing motor boat and butty. Construction could be in wood and card or from plastic card. The kits and drawings mentioned above are typical narrow boats but there were many variations in design, both regional to suit the width and depth of canals and locks on particular systems and structural to accommodate varying types of cargo. The modeller prepared to scratchbuild might like to repre-

sent different types of canal boat to add variety and interest to the scene.

The narrow canals are the best known and, because they do not require much space, are perhaps the most convenient to model for a railway layout. However, there are two other wider types of waterway, the barge or broad canals and the ship canals. The latter are really too large for inclusion on most layouts but a section of broad canal could be modelled, particularly if the layout represented an industrial area. This would allow the introduction of a wider range of canal craft, many of which are very interesting. The Skinley range of 4mm scale ship model drawings include craft suitable for these wider canals, including some barges. To anyone who would like to see just how varied and interesting the canal craft can be I would recommend *Britain's Canal & River Craft* by E. Paget-Tomlinson (Moorland Publishing Co Ltd). The excellent sketches in this book would also be very helpful to the modeller who would like to scratchbuild examples for a canal scene on a model railway layout.

I have illustrated this article with photographs of several model canals on railway layouts but I would suggest that you look at real canals to gain further ideas and information before planning and building your own model. A canal scene will add greatly to the scenic interest of a layout whether it is only a short stretch or a major feature, so why not consider including one on your next layout?

Model a miniature railway

Michael Andress

Miniature railways are usually classed as lines of from 7¼in to 24in gauge on which the motive power takes the form of models of steam or diesel locomotives rather than being full size, though narrow gauge, prototypes. Throughout Britain there are many of these passenger carrying railways. They are mainly to be found in tourist areas where they are very popular with holiday-makers both young and old. Two typical examples of these miniature railways are shown in the accompanying photographs.

A model of such a line can be an interesting and very appropriate scenic addition to a model railway layout. On a large exhibition layout in 00 scale constructed by members of the Isle of Purbeck Model Railway Club the main station was based on Dawlish, with the railway running beside the sea and beach. Terry Jenkins built a model of a miniature railway on the promenade which lies alongside but below the level of the station. This was a simple non-working model but the little line attracted a great deal of interest as an unusual scenic feature.

The locomotive, the 4-2-2 *Lord of the Isles*, was from a series of small plastic models of engines, cars, etc, sold mounted on pencil sharpeners. Terry removed it from the sharpener and repaint-

ed it in appropriate Great Western Railway colours. There was no tender provided but this was easily modelled from balsa wood and card, painted to match the locomotive and fitted with a 4mm scale sitting figure to represent the driver. The locomotive is 40mm long and the tender 25mm. Each coach has a body made from a 56mm length of ⅜in square hard balsa stripwood with a strip ⅜in × 1/16in glued to the top for the clerestory. The bogies were represented by small blocks of wood. The coach bodies were painted matt black at this stage, then paper sides painted in cream and brown with windows in black fixed to each side of the wooden bodies. Alternatively the coaches could be modelled hollowed out so that the passengers could sit in them rather than on top.

The surface of the promenade was covered with embossed card sheeting representing grey stone so Terry simply painted silver lines on this to simulate rails inset into the promenade. At other sites where sleepers would be visible these could be drawn out and rails of thin plastic strip or rod glued down onto them. Miniature railways usually have a shed or more elaborate building in which the locomotive or locomotives and rolling stock can be stored when not in use and where main-

The Ravenglass & Eskdale Railway in Cumberland is one of Britain's best known miniature railways, operating on 15 inch gauge. River Esk a freelance 2-8-2 built in 1923 has just arrived at Ravenglass and is waiting to be turned for another trip.

This diesel outline locomotive of freelance design running on the Poole Park 10¼ inch gauge line is powered by a Ford 10 petrol engine; note the typical cut away section to accommodate the driver.

Left *The model miniature railway built by Terry Jenkins, on the promenade below the model full size station adds interest to the scene.*

Left *Another view of the line showing also the realistically modelled beach and groyne.*

Left *Terry Jenkins used a model from a pencil sharpener for the locomotive and scratchbuilt the tender and coaches from odds and ends of wood and card.*

Below left *The locomotive and stock storage shed and workshop was built from a Bilteezi card kit.*

tenance and repairs can be carried out. Terry used a model from the Bilteezi colour printed card kit series to serve this purpose on his line. Many miniature railways have other structures, station building, platform, signal box, signals, footbridge, and so on, and these could be modelled from scratch or modified from suitable commercially available models or kits if you wish to add them.

Such a non-working model of a miniature railway can be constructed very easily but will be a most interesting scenic feature on a layout. However, working models have also been produced. P.D. Hancock is well known as a pioneer in 4mm scale narrow gauge modelling. An ingenious and

imaginative modeller he actually installed a working miniature railway in the garden of one of the
houses on his 4mm scale 'Craig & Mertonford
Railway'. The garden railway is in fact a small
clockwork toy of German manufacture. Beneath
the oval of track, in reality a continuous oval slot,
is an elastic band which passes around two
pulleys, one of which is directly driven by the
clockwork motor. Tags on the elastic band link
with projecting pins beneath the locomotive and

coaches so that the train runs around the oval.
The toy has been skilfully blended into the
scenery of the layout and the resulting effect is
very good. Because the scale is approximately
½mm to the foot the modeller has described it as
'Quintublo'.

Two other modellers, Ron Prattley and Dave
Howson, also tackled the subject with imagination and ingenuity but with a very different
approach. It occurred to them that in 1/32 scale

*The working garden railway on P.
D. Hancock's famous 'Craig &
Mertonford Railway' 4mm scale
narrow gauge layout. (Photograph
by courtesy of P. D. Hancock).*

*An overall view of the garden, com-
plete with 10¼ inch gauge miniature railway, modelled in 1/32 scale
by Dave Howson and Ron Prattley.
The layout measures 4 ft by 2 ft and
the controls are concealed by the
low relief bungalow.*

*The oval track layout has a passing
loop at the station with a siding
leading to the workshop in the
garage of the bungalow. The locomotives are standard N scale
models and the coach was built
from a Highfield kit modified to
provide seating for the driver and
passengers.*

Two further views of the 'Garden of Eden' layout built by Ron Prattley and Dave Howson. Note the many flowers, plants and other garden details, mainly from the Britains range, which have been added to create a very interesting and realistic model. (Both photographs by Ron Prattley).

9mm track (N gauge) was approximately equivalent to 10¼ in gauge. Thus the idea of modelling a 10¼ in garden railway using 9mm track with N scale locomotives and rolling stock combined with Britains 1/32 scale figures and garden accessories was developed. The completed layout measured 4ft × 2ft and represented a garden complete with miniature railway, greenhouse, cold frame, ornamental pond, lawn, trellis, flower beds and vegetable patch. One wall of the bungalow was modelled at one end of the layout and served also to conceal the controls. The track plan was very simple but the unusual theme and presentation together with the realistic modelling of the garden made the layout very effective and it created considerable interest whenever exhibited. The 'Garden of Eden' layout as it was named was featured in the September 1970 issue of *Model Railway Constructor* magazine. With the availability now of Z scale models it is worth noting that in 7mm scale Z gauge track would similarly be approximately equivalent to 10¼ in gauge.

Though rarely represented a miniature railway can be very effective in model form, as illustrated by these examples, so if you have a little space to spare on your layout why not instal one for your miniature enthusiasts?